CW01667980

Lent with John Donne

A spiritual pilgrimage to the cross through sacred writings by John Donne

Curated by Fr Tim Clayton

The Annunciation and Passion
The Collect for Good Friday
HOLY SATURDAY
Holy Sonnet XII
Holy Sonnet XIV

If I were but mere dust and ashes...

Holy Meditation I.

Lent with John Donne
A spiritual pilgrimage to the cross through sacred writings
by John Donne

Trinity Books

An imprint of Trinity North Shore
on Boston's North Shore

www.trinitynorthshore.org

Works selected, introduction, invitation, and editorial text by
Fr Timothy Clayton.

Editorial assistance by Alex Miller.

ISBN: 979-8-9868161-1-1

Printed in USA.

First edition.

TABLE of CONTENTS

APOLOGIA

My love of the John Donne began the first time I visited Oxford.[1] The City of Dreaming Spires had already begun to work its magic, but it was Blackwell's on Broad Street[2] that I thought must surely have pearly gates, being the largest bookstore on planet Earth. I headed for the basement, for the

---

[1] Some who enjoyed *Christmas with John Donne* have asked how I came to be so enamored of the man. So, with sincere apologies, here is the story.

[2] For the record, that's BH Blackwell Ltd, 48 to 51 Broad Street, Oxford. The bookmark I saved from a subsequent visit-and-inevitable-purchase also includes this lovely poem about the bookseller:

> Happy the morning giving time to stop
> An hour at once in Basil Blackwell's shop
> There, in the Broad, within whose booky house
> Half England's scholars nibble books or browse.
> Where'er they wander blessed fortune theirs:
> Books to the ceiling, other books upstairs;
> Books, doubtless, in the cellar, and behind
> Romantic bays, where iron ladders wind.
>
> John Masefield

Masefield was England's Poet Laureate from 1930 to 1967. His poem celebrating Blackwell's is from 1941.

used section, seeing as how I was a graduate student with a wife pregnant with our second, and our first such a wee toddler that her favorite experience in all of Oxford was the echo which she rather loudly discovered she could command in the Sheldonian Theatre.

But I was determined to come away with some prize, and indeed I did. I came away with Penguin Classics' *The Complete English Poems of John Donne*, a curious figure I knew only remotely but heard had been a living fire. Alas, however, we returned home, the summer ended, the semester began, and our next child arrived. All good and right, even wonderful, but they did add up to mean that the Donne book languished on my shelf, neglected.

At last, I made a start several years later when following an academic conference in England I joined a few friends at a cabin in Wales. It was November; the last night I was there sleep was elusive as the winds rattled the shutters and screeched ominously around the window edges. No big deal, surely; just Celtic and perfectly *de rigeur* heading into late autumn.

I was wrong. It was a 500 (or something)-year-level flood. I needed to get to London to talk with a professor I hoped would take me under his wing;

however, as it turned out, the trains had been flooded out – a possibility I had not considered, as I had an idyllic, yeah romantic, view of train travel on this, the far side of the Great Pond. But due to my naïveté, my South African and Canadian friend and I headed to town, and the car got flooded out in a massive waterlog in a curve we encountered at the same moment as a massive, double-decker bus coming from the opposite direction.

Thanks to some helpful local farmers who probably to this day make merry over their ales in remembering the gents with more book learning than common sense, we finally made it to Machynlleth. There I learned the fate of the trains and of my friend's car: water and electronics do not mix well, and it was, per the slang of those days said, "toast". I caught a bus to Aberystwyth, rented the last car available, and began to wind through lovely rural Wales, occasionally getting lost in the midst of small towns whose unpronounceable names had about seven 'l's in them.

Eventually, I found the M4 and on to London, far too late of course for my meeting with the professor. But all was not lost; away back in the lovely little book shop in Machnylleth I at least had enough foresight to secure a roadmap. Ah, yes, and something for the drive: an audiobook of Richard

Burton reading the love sonnets of John Donne, a classic, apparently, recorded in 1958.

And so it began. Soon thereafter I got the languishing book purchased that bucolic summer's holiday in Oxford down from the shelf, thinking some of these love sonnets would come in handy with my delightful wife. And then I discovered La Corona. Love sonnets, indeed.

What I offer you here, I do hope, is the ongoing joy of this discovery, turned to the purpose of what is to me life's greatest discovery. And that will involve a pilgrimage...

INVITATION and ORIENTATION to PILGRIMAGE

I suppose no one knows how many people have walked the *Via Dolorosa*, the Way of Suffering, tracing the path of Jesus carrying his Cross to his Passion, but I suspect all can agree that the number is not a small one, collective distances traveled from so many spots on the globe. I wonder how many of those who have walked it have realized that they were on pilgrimage? Many did, certainly.

This book is a pilgrimage – a spiritual pilgrimage, granted, but a pilgrimage nonetheless – to the Cross, through the season of Lent. The ancient custom of pilgrimage generally seems to be having a revival of late, something I take as happy news. Pilgrimage is a route, a time and an effort — a journey — to a sacred place for the purpose of drawing nearer to God both in the meaning present in the destination but also along the way as well: the setting apart of the necessary expenditures of all types — time, attention, other opportunities, whatever it is — doing its own bit to enable us the more deeply to appreciate and bring into ourselves whatever that meaning is, and to meet our God along the way. Or perhaps it would be more apt to say we put ourselves in a position to be met *by* our God the more deeply at the destination for having cleared our calendars, our desks, and our devices, and thus freed our attention to be available. And we expect God graciously to carry us along the way, ever-present, whether we sense him there or not.

For those who pilgrimaged with us through *Christmas with John Donne*, this pilgrimage will be a little different: we will appoint some readings to days that they thematically fit. Ash Wednesday, for instance, is a singular day in the whole of the church calendar. So also Good Friday. Holy Week itself has a focus and is set apart. I have not gone so far as to dole out a daily reading, and certainly each of the readings is worthwhile whether or not you manage them on the suggested day. Should you discover this book in the midst of Lent, no worries. But it is worth beginning with the readings for Ash Wednesday (Holy Sonnet I and Divine Meditation I) because the introduction to each of them sets up each of those two genres, and we will have several of both Donne's Holy Sonnets and his Divine Meditations as we journey along.

Finally, you may notice that many of our

readings were not written by Donne explicitly for Lent or the day to which I have appointed them (some were); nonetheless thematically they (I believe) fit, and fit quite well. As a matter of fact, there is no shortage of Donne's sacred works that would fit, given both the poignant awareness in his era of our human frailty and mortality and also given the emphasis on the holiness and transcendence of God.

So welcome to this Lenten pilgrimage, a spiritual pilgrimage to the Cross. Yes, there is strong medicine here, but also there is soul food for the journey, and for the living these forty days and beyond. Therefore, as you begin, dear fellow pilgrim:

> May you find in this small volume a time and space set apart where God draws near and leads you in his love to face whatever it is you need to face, for your healing and for your knowing deeply that, in spite of it all, God's mercy and love are real, and are for you.

Tim+

INTRODUCTION to JOHN DONNE: PROMETHEAN FIRE

Perhaps you know John Donne for his romantic sonnets or his stubbornly resilient reputation as a prolific and rather free lover, who boasted of the variety of his romantic conquests. Or perhaps for "no man is an island" or "ask not for whom the bell tolls" or some other snippet that has embedded itself doggedly into your imagination from the days of high school literature class. Perhaps from his rakish pose which hangs in the National Portrait Gallery in London, mustachioed, insouciant, self-assured, debonair under a black hat with an excessive brim. Or perhaps you noted the sculpted statue of him while touring St Paul's Cathedral on a visit to London and recall the remarkable fact that it was the only monument in that great church to survive the Great Fire of 1666.

That Donne's monument should have survived the Fire is fitting, in its own fittingly figurative way: fire cannot destroy fire.

"Wit" was the vogue of the seventeenth century, in pub and parlor, in poetry and rhetoric. The great art of wit was to replace the conventions of regular meter or rhyme schemes with deft paradoxes of insight and cleverly surprising turns that would catch the reader's or hearer's anticipation off guard. The more disparate the comparison, the more eccentric the analogy, the farther the paradox stretched the imagination, the greater the "conceit" the poet or orator achieved, the better.

Wit was the vogue, and John Donne was its master. The introduction to the Oxford World's Classics volume of Donne's works begins:

> John Donne was a new kind of poet. His originality was what impressed contemporaries. It seemed to them that he had changed the literary universe. He was 'Copernicus in poetry' — a Promethean innovator, who had done away with the 'pedantic weeds' and musty trappings of classical mythology. No English poet had been so avant-garde before. Nor had any English poet been so intellectual or so difficult... Admirers commemorated him at his death in images of power and energy. He had

reigned over the 'monarchy of wit'; an 'awful fire' had burned in his 'clear brain'.[3]

"Nor had any English poet been so intellectual or so difficult..." Perhaps this puts many would-be readers off Donne. He may take a second or even a third (or fourth) reading – the author of a fantastically-entertaining new biography of him puts it well, "he could write a twelve-line sonnet that would take you a week to read,"[4] but the return is well worth the investment.

---

[3] John Carey (ed. and introduction), *John Donne, The Major Works, including Song and Sonnets and sermons* (Oxford World's Classics, Oxford University Press, 2000), xix.

[4] This refreshing acknowledgment that even the brilliant have to re-read Donne is on p. 258 of Katherine Rundell's *Super-Infinite, The Transformations of John Donne* (Farrar, Straus, and Giroux, 2022). If I may say, should this book (that you are reading now) brings you any pleasure or edification, do read Rundell's biography.

She also offers a worthwhile critique of the basically assumed view that Donne turned to the Anglican faith only as a social expedient, and then, later, did the same again of economic necessity in presenting himself for ordination to the priesthood.

I have never found that assumption convincing: yes, humans are complex, with multiple layers of motivations. And yes, I do love Donne's rather, ahem, forward love sonnets (apologies, O chaste reader), but when one reads the

Certainly, wit, intellect, an older form of English, different mores of society, and all the rest accepted as barriers, yes – but, nonetheless, Donne is a voice for all times, surely, and poignantly a voice for ours. The reality is that for all his brilliance and his reputation, for all his posturing and brazen confidence, he also knew loss, grief, anxiety, depression; knew his world fallen apart, all things in flux, nothing assured, and perhaps, therefore, an insatiable longing for connection, in physical intimacy and beyond, to the mystical, spiritual, eternal. It all comes together poignantly in his funeral orations, along with the frequent use of the rather strong word "putrefy" and its cousins. Good heavens.

Holy Sonnets of his later life one finds the same passion, now directed to a new (and what theology would call a deeper) consummation. And, certainly, he committed himself to studying the theology of it all.

No; it is a bit like what I think I remember Bono once remarked of Van Morrison: something about noticing that in his youth Van sang about girls, but later he sang about God. But he is the same Van Morrison, with the same ache driving the same creativity and genius.

At any rate, Rundell's treatment of the question is in her chapter "The Clergyman", especially beginning on p. 210, "But Donne had been hunting for God since his thirties."

Donne is particularly well-suited as a companion for Lent, having faced life's hard realities. He suffered deeply personal losses, knew grief intimately, and wondered if anything is solid, real, or trustworthy: whether anything abides. I have included a longish set of excerpts from a sermon on the book of Job, for instance: the sermon is just too poignant for frequent interruptions.

He found hope in the most profound act of love known to humankind: when one gave his own life for his friends. And that voluntarily, with humble and quiet acceptance, no posturing, the furthest thing from the vogue arrogance of Donne's own day. Donne's sacred writings of each genre — poetry, prayers, meditations, sermons — on this amazing love are refreshingly honest. His confessions read to us as embarrassingly stringent if anything. His sermons allow, rather than repress, the poet's genius of image, figure of speech, emotion, and passion.

Finally, do not be intimidated by the prospect of reading the King's English. There is an argument to be made that it is simpler, actually, than the way we speak — the meaning of words more clear and the logical construction of the grammar more consistent. At any rate, though wit and its conceits were the fashion of the day, their use of English was not pretentious; it was simply communication at that time. Relax and enjoy it; a rhythm will come.

ASH WEDNESDAY

I have sometimes referred to the sacristy of a church as the "locker room". I intend no irreverence; it is a holy space, filled with the vestments, vessels, and various accouterments of the more sacramental churches, with our church calendar and its seasons, and our emphasis on including the tactile in worship. By that nickname for that space, I am not intending to make common that which is sacred, but I am referencing the camaraderie in service of priests and lay servers. It takes me back to high school soccer: you come in from the joys or challenges of the day, change out of the styles of the times and your own expression of them to be absorbed into the commonality of a uniform, come together and discuss the particulars and note the roles involved in the ordered activity you are about to engage, and focus. Even on the soccer team, we would join in the Our Father before each match.

I have noticed over the years that the atmosphere in that sort of holy locker room is different on Ash Wednesdays. A touch of it comes with any weekday evening service: there are always those lay folks who have arrived a bit frazzled, having heroically fought the good fight against the powers and dominions of traffic on the highways. But it is more than that. It would be too much to say everyone is anxious or on edge, but there is that little something, just under the surface: there is a sobriety that comes of the anticipation of marking people with a reminder of what their bodies one day will become, of what they will cease to be.

Ash Wednesday is the one day of the year in the church's calendar which is dedicated to the facing of our mortality and is the first bookend of the most somber of all the days in the church's calendar. To be fair, this does not make the church dour: once a year is not frequent, and if we are honest we have to admit that we in the developed, savvy West spend a fair amount of energy on the denial of our finitude. Still, it may be to our good but that does not make it pleasant to administer. And much less fun to mark the sign of the cross on an infant — a tender, fresh life and hope presented at the altar in the arms of a new mother, perhaps only recently delivered; it feels like a shattering of innocence, a cruel act, begrudgingly them their joy. Nor to mark the terminally ill: it seems almost a mockery of what they know already and carry every day. And the elderly: some have made their peace, not to say have surrendered to the inevitable nor quite resigned themselves, but simply come to a place where they are not in denial, even subconsciously, but for others it is a particularly poignant reminder that the clock is ticking, after all.

In one church I served we had a tough, resilient woman who had faced a series of medical challenges and now was in a battle with what would be terminal cancer. One Ash Wednesday she knelt at the rail beside a much-loved and thriving professor from the local college, the sort to whose office students flocked, drawn by his effervescent *joie de vivre*. Two weeks later he was gone from a heart attack, and yet she fought on, disturbed by the seeming absurdity of it all.

Naturally, these are realities we would rather ignore. Some years there is another twist: Ash Wednesday falls on February 14th. It will happen the year after this book's publication (2024). No one wants to hear it, but on the occasion of that particular confluence of days we are forced to consider that to love deeply and share the years — should romance lead to life-long, covenant commitment — then one of us will be loving the other through their end and will know grief more deeply than we can imagine.

Perhaps I am laying it on a bit thick. But then again, Ash Wednesday calls for that: it is but one day of the entire year given over to facing a reality that is as universal as it is inevitable. Death is not called "ultimate" for nothing.

And certainly, in Donne's times, people knew their finitude; human mortality was not hidden nor sanitarily managed. Epidemics did not surprise them. All had suffered the loss of loved ones at some personal level, to some cause or other.

Death was so near that though this sonnet and meditation were not written specifically for Ash Wednesday, they well could have been. John Donne was all too familiar with death, and its cost was dear to him throughout his life. It began early; his father died when he was but a young lad, aged four. Two of Anne's and his children were stillborn. Another three died before they were aged ten. Seven survived their first decade, just over half.

Perhaps it was the cumulative effect of these losses that led Donne to write a defense of suicide. Happily, he never published it, and, much more happily, he drew back from the edge himself. But his dear Anne died nine years later, five days after giving birth to her twelfth child, who was stillborn. Donne mourned her deeply, as any husband would, but also surely intensified by his profound depth of feeling and his insight via experience into the incongruity of it all.

Donne wrote the seventeenth of his series of Holy Sonnets of his grief at Anne's death, and the beginning speaks to the effect it had on him:

> Since she whom I lov'd hath paid her last debt
> To nature, and to hers, and my good is dead,
> And her soul early into heaven ravished,
> Wholly in heavenly things my mind is set.

That (!) from Donne, famous lover, the same one who earlier in life had written a very different sort of poem, The Indifferent:

> I can love both fair and brown,
> Her whom abundance melts, and her whom want betrays,
> Her who loves loneness best, and her who masks and plays,
> Her whom the country formed, and whom the town,
> Her who believes, and her who tries,
> Her who still weeps with spongy eyes,
> And her who is dry cork, and never cries;
> I can love her, and her, and you, and you,
> I can love any, so she be not true.

Later in our pilgrimage we will see Donne regret and repent of this attitude. But, for now what we want to notice is simply this: grief had its effect.

And so it is here that we begin, with the first bookend of the two most sobering of all the days marked on the church's calendar, the bookends being completed by Good Friday — the two days paired by the vestments of the sacred liturgy being black, what with death being their theme.

Holy Sonnet I

Donne wrote a series of Holy Sonnets. In what manner or to what degree they are meant to be connected is, as far as I can sort it, still debated. But I will venture this much: it would be surprising had Donne passed by the opportunity to show his genius by intricately and subtly connecting them in a progression. I find they work best if read in sequence, even if in no sense greater than simply creating an ethos.

Whatever it is, having said that I now must break the hard news that we are not quite taking them in sequence. We will take a core of them in sequence later, Holy Sonnets II-IX, but this one, the first, is just too *à propos* to Ash Wednesday to set elsewhere. The same, I will suggest later, is, in varying degrees, true for each of Holy Sonnets X-XIV, which will be set during Holy Week, on certain days appropriate to each.

But today, Ash Wednesday, Holy Sonnet I sets

the very first step of our pilgrimage as a poignant question: the opening line of this sonnet probes the incongruity of death. The line can be read from different angles: is it born of Donne's fiercely independent spirit? An implicit complaint-critique directed at God? Or perhaps it is lament shared with God that God's handiwork should come to this, to death and dissolution? At any rate, it is, of course, naming a poignantly ironic incongruity, to which the rest of the sonnet is a response.

The last line has a word that is no longer in use and therefore may make the image difficult to grasp. *Adamant* or *adamantine* in the ancient world is the word from which our word *diamond* derived and comes from the Greek meaning *unconquerable* or *untameable* (the Greek negation called an alpha privative attached to the word for power or might — *dunamis*, like *dynamic*). But somewhere in the Middle Ages it was, apparently, confusedly connected with the naturally magnetic rock lodestone, and, separately, to the Latin word *adamare*, meaning *to love, to be attached to*. And that — Donne praying that his heart would love God passionately — is very much who he was, and a suiting way both to begin Lent, and to respond to the question which will lead us into our pilgrimage through Lent, the question of the incongruity of death.

Thou hast made me, and shall thy work decay?
Repair me now, for now mine end doth haste,
I run to death, and death meets me as fast,
And all my pleasures are like yesterday,
I dare not move my dim eyes any way,
Despair behind, and death before doth cast
Such terror, and my feebled flesh doth waste
By sin in it, which it towards hell doth weigh;
Only thou art above, and when towards thee
By thy leave I can look, I rise again
But our old subtle foe so tempteth me,
That not one hour I can myself sustain,
Thy grace may wing me to prevent his art,
And thou like adamant draw mine iron heart.

Perhaps in later readings, after familiarity has been established, it may be worth reading the sonnet with an eye to a subtle pattern: the first half of the poem walks us into a gathering sense of hopelessness, culminating as the last line of the upper half, line seven, and the first line of the lower half, line eight, of the poem couple to give a poignant "yes" in response to the opening question — the effect being a dark, seemingly irresistible inevitability, relentlessly pulling us, despite all our resistance:

> Thou hast made me, and shall thy work decay?
> ...
> Such terror, and my feebled flesh doth waste
> By sin in it, which it towards hell doth weigh.

But then, surprise!, the lower half thematically answers the upper, in reverse order, or in matching order if considered from the center out. Take your time, read this like a large U, down the left side, across the two in the middle, and then up the right side, and noting the thematic similarities in each row (across the columns). My personal favorite is the paired lines five and six with the paired lines nine and ten: when we have been boxed in before and behind, nowhere else to go, unable to move, still

God is above, in another dimension and opening a horizon, should we look where it is not fearful to move one's eyes — towards him.

Thou hast made me, and shall thy work decay?
Repair me now, for now mine end doth haste,
I run to death, and death meets me as fast,
And all my pleasures are like yesterday,
I dare not move my dim eyes any way,
Despair behind, and death before doth cast

And thou like adamant draw mine iron heart.
Thy grace may wing me to prevent his art,
That not one hour I can myself sustain,
But our old subtle foe so tempteth me,
By thy leave I can look, I rise again
Only thou art above, and when towards thee

Such terror, and my feebled flesh doth waste
By sin in it, which it towards hell doth weigh

The sonnet sets for us the question of this Lent: shall God's work decay, enfeebled and drawn as if by an evil tractor beam down and ever down? Or will the acts and grace of God lift us, working love in our hearts, desiring to connect to him, and pulling us as if magnetically, as if using the very hardness of our hearts by some paradoxical majesty of grace, pure gift, to draw us to himself?

Devotion I.

INSULTUS MORBI PRIMUS.

The first Alteration, the first Grudging, of the Sickness.

In the winter 1623, Donne fell into a sudden and grave illness. Many think that it was likely from an epidemic of typhus, which was loose and during that period killed perhaps hundreds of thousands across England, but others point out that the symptoms he described could have indicated other diseases that were rampant as well. Donne was 52. His head felt as if it were splitting, his fever spiked, his body bore spots and sores. In bed he felt so weak that in the third meditation he wrote that it felt as if "my slack sinews are iron fetters, and those thin sheets iron doors upon me." He grew so weary of the bed, filled as mattresses were in those days with feathers, that he cried out: "As thou hast made these feathers thorns, in the sharpness of this sickness, so, Lord, make these thorns feathers again."

He insisted on a pen and paper (of course) to find some kind of release. He wrote a series of twenty-three meditations, it was said with deeply-focused concentration and incredible speed. As they say, death has a way of focusing the mind. Late that same year, and after recovering, he published them as *Devotions upon Emergent Occasions.* They were published in January of 1624, and then again in 1634 and 1638.

Each of the twenty-three meditations is in three parts: Meditation, Expostulation, and ending with a Prayer. The full title is worth seeing:

DEVOTIONS
UPON
Emergent Occasions and serval steps in my Sickness

Digested into

I. Meditations *upon our Humane Condition.*

II. Espostulations, *and Debatements with God.*

III. Prayers, *upon the several occasions, to him.*

To us a strange word, *debatements* — seeming overly-formal, the kind of thing that when the children were little we pretended our huge goofy dog would say when trying to sound intellectual, all in silly fun. But of course, we realize what it means, and there is nothing silly about it; it is painfully real. For us it is also an invitation and a help. Dear friends, bring your *debatements* with God along on our pilgrimage: add them with the baggage of sins and failures, which we shall confess and be released to shed as we go, but let God sort this baggage. At the end perhaps we will be able to lay it at the Cross.

Our readings will be excerpts from selected ones of the twenty-three Meditations, and I have taken the liberty of dividing some of Donne's longer paragraphs for easier comprehension and digestion.

A quick word of content warning: some of this is perhaps distasteful to our sensibilities. Death, disease, loss, and grief were not strangers to Donne or his era, and they spoke frankly about them, with less careful delicacy than we typically expect. Donne, as we have said, knew much loss himself and in part he is sharing his own working out of how these things must be (just *must* be, for they simply *are*, horrible as they are).

But also he is later in his life now, and despite of falling suddenly ill himself, he is, in some of these, sharing where he had found that hope lies. Some of that will be subtle, some more clear, in various of the meditations we will meet.

Overall, I consider this strong medicine: hard to swallow but necessary if we are to face reality. I take that to be what Ash Wednesday, itself, is basically about. And so, we begin with the first meditation not only because it is the first, but for reasons that I trust will be apparent. Whatever you do with this piece, do not miss the Expostulation: a poet's figurative imagination sneaking powerfully in, to color even an exasperated complaint, and that Prayer, good heavens, it gives me shivers...

MEDITATION.

Variable, and therefore miserable condition of man! this minute I was well, and am ill, this minute. I am surprised with a sudden change, and alteration to worse, and can impute it to no cause, nor call it by any name. We study health, and we deliberate upon our meats, and drink, and air, and exercises, and we hew and we polish every stone that goes to that building; and so our health is a long and a regular work: but in a minute a cannon batters all, overthrows all, demolishes all; a sickness unprevented for all our diligence, unsuspected for all our curiosity; nay, undeserved, if we consider only disorder, summons us, seizes us, possesses us, destroys us in an instant.

O miserable condition of man! which was not imprinted by God, who, as he is immortal himself, had put a coal, a beam of immortality into us, which we might have blown into a flame, but blew it out by our first sin; we beggared ourselves by hearkening after false riches, and infatuated ourselves by hearkening after false knowledge...

Is this the honour which man hath by being a little world, that he hath these earthquakes in himself, sudden shakings; these lightnings, sudden flashes; these thunders, sudden noises; these eclipses, sudden offuscations and darkening of his senses; these blazing stars, sudden fiery exhalations; these rivers of blood, sudden red waters? Is he a world to himself only therefore, that he hath enough in himself, not only to destroy and execute himself, but to presage that execution upon himself; to assist the sickness, to antedate the sickness, to make the sickness the more irremediable by sad apprehensions, and, as if he would make a fire the more vehement by sprinkling water upon the coals, so to wrap a hot fever in cold melancholy, lest the fever alone should not destroy fast enough without this contribution, nor perfect the work (which is destruction) except we joined an artificial sickness of our own melancholy, to our natural, our unnatural fever. O perplexed discomposition, O riddling distemper, O miserable condition of man!

EXPOSTULATION.

If I were but mere dust and ashes I might speak unto the Lord, for the Lord's hand made me of this dust, and the Lord's hand shall re-collect these ashes; the Lord's hand was the wheel upon which this vessel of clay was framed, and the Lord's hand is the urn in which these ashes shall be preserved. I am the dust and the ashes of the temple of the Holy Ghost, and what marble is so precious? But I am more than dust and ashes: I am my best part, I am my soul. And being so, the breath of God, I may breathe back these pious expostulations to my God...

PRAYER.

O eternal and most gracious God, who, considered in thyself, art a circle, first and last, and altogether; but, considered in thy working upon us, art a direct line, and leadest us from our beginning, through all our ways, to our end, enable me by thy grace to look forward to mine end, and to look backward too, to the considerations of thy mercies afforded me from the beginning; that so by that practice of considering thy mercy, in my beginning in this world, when thou plantedst me in the Christian church, and thy mercy in the beginning in the other world, when thou writest me in the book of life, in my election, I may come to a holy consideration of thy mercy in the beginning of all my actions here... but keep me still established, both in a constant assurance, that thou wilt speak to me at the beginning of every such sickness, at the approach of every such sin; and that, if I take knowledge of that voice then, and fly to thee, thou wilt preserve me from falling, or raise me again, when by natural infirmity I am fallen. Do this, O Lord, for his sake, who knows our natural infirmities, for he had them, and knows the weight of our sins, for he paid a dear price for them, thy Son, our Saviour, Christ Jesus. Amen.

The Psalm and Collect for the First Day of Lent
(Ash Wednesday)

These are from the Book of Common Prayer that would have been in use during Donne's years as priest, with the spelling updated to what is common for our day.

The First Day of Lent

Domine ne. Psalm vi.

O LORD rebuke me not in thine indignation: neither chasten me in thy displeasure.
Have mercy upon me, O Lord, for I am weak, O Lord, heal me, my bones are vexed.
My soul also is sore troubled: but Lord, how long wilt thou punish me?
Turn thee, O Lord, and deliver my soul: Oh save me for thy mercies sake.
For in death no man remembreth thee and who will give the thanks in the pit?
I am weary of my groaning; every night wash I my bed: and water my couch with my tears.
My beauty is gone for very trouble: and worn away because of all mine enemies.
Away from me, all ye that work vanity: for the Lord hath heard the voice of my weeping.
The Lord hath heard my petition: the Lord will receive my prayer.
All mine enemies shall be confounded, and sore vexed: they shall be turned back, and put to shame suddenly.
Glory be to the father, &c.
As it was in the beginning, &c.

The Collect.

ALMIGHTY and everlasting God, which hatest nothing that thou hast made, and dost forgive the sins of all them that be penitent; Create and make in us new and contrite hearts, that we worthily lamenting our sins, and acknowledging our wretchedness, may obtain of thee, the God of all mercy, perfect remission and forgiveness; through Jesus Christ.

LENT

Lent is the primary penitential season in the Church's calendar. It is a time of holy self-reflection and for that perhaps most elusive thing of all, deep self-honesty. I always remind people that this is a limited, focused time within the life of the Church: this acute focus on penitential self-honesty is made more possible because we walk into it aware that we are held by the secure mercy and love of God. We take heart because its purpose is not our humiliation but rather our redemption into all that we were always meant to be, into the eventual finding of our true selves by revealing more and more and giving it over to Jesus as a death of the illusions in which we have wrapped our story of ourselves, and an awakening in us of the life and Spirit of Jesus.

Of course, Lent began yesterday, on Ash Wednesday, and continues for forty days, not counting Sundays (which are days of the resurrection) and ending with dusk on Maundy Thursday. The next three days — Good Friday,

Holy Saturday, and Easter Sunday — are the Holy Triduum, the Holy Three Days.

For our purposes here we mean the days of Lent after Ash Wednesday and before Holy Week. We will give each day of Holy Week (starting with Palm Sunday) readings especially suited to that time when the events walk in step with the biblical story of Jesus' Passion.

Here we will walk through the core of Donne's Holy Sonnets (II-IX), through excerpts of four of his Divine Meditations, with a hymn of confession, and through excerpts of three (rather amazing) sermons, including his last sermon, when he was facing his own death, and known as Death's Duel.

Depending on how you take the sermons — whether in one long sitting or perhaps one excerpt a day — there are enough readings here to give not quite one a day, so call it almost daily but with also with built-in time for catching up, and not to require a stressful pace.

We begin with the Holy Sonnets.

Holy Sonnet II

Donne here lists a lovely summary litany of God's work for and in us. He then turns to the struggles he faces, and he faces a fear he carries. Much humility here, and acknowledgment of our weakness and need of God's mercy and grace.

As due by many titles I resign
Myself to thee, O God. First I was made
By Thee; and for Thee, and when I was decay'd
Thy blood bought that, the which before was thine.
I am Thy son, made with Thyself to shine,
Thy servant, whose pains Thou hast still repaid,
Thy sheep, Thine image, and—till I betray'd
Myself—a temple of Thy Spirit divine;
Why doth the devil then usurp on me?
Why doth he steal, nay ravish, that's Thy right?
Except Thou rise and for Thine own work fight,
O! I shall soon despair, when I shall see
That Thou lovest mankind well, yet wilt not choose me,
And Satan hates me, yet is loth to lose me.

Holy Sonnet III

This sonnet is highly confessional. It begins with a worthy plea: that Donne might weep as much over his sin and its opportunity costs as he wept in his wilder days, perhaps over love affairs or under the influence of an abundance of alcohol.

This sonnet is an instance where we see a less-delicate era's assumption of a direct correlation of sin and at least some subsequent suffering. But perhaps we should not be too quick to judge: perhaps Donne is not suggesting a vengeful God, but, rather, simply that he made life and love difficult for himself and that had consequences naturally (we may say).

O! might those sighs and tears return again
Into my breast and eyes, which I have spent,
That I might in this holy discontent
Mourn with some fruit, as I have mourn'd in vain;
In mine idolatry what showers of rain
Mine eyes did waste? what griefs my heart did rent?
That sufferance was my sin, I now repent,
'Cause I did suffer, I must suffer pain.
Th'hydroptic drunkard, and night-scouting thief,
The itchy lecher, and self-tickling proud
Have the remembrance of past joys, for relief
Of coming ills. To poor me is allow'd
No ease; for long, yet vehement grief hath been
Th' effect and cause, the punishment and sin.

Holy Sonnet IV

I am tempted already to remind us all that I forewarned us (I need to hear it too!) that Lent is strong medicine, and Donne sometimes serves it in rather tart spoonfuls. But I read this one as him wrestling his distracted, unruly soul down, in order to give attention to what is real and true. He is determined to take that soul there until it — against its strong wishes — responds appropriately. Let us remember that Donne is no less passionate or dramatic in his love poems, say; it is simply him, and why we love him.

O, my black Soul! now thou art summoned
By sickness, death's herald and champion;
Thou art like a pilgrim, which abroad hath done
Treason, and durst not turn to whence he's fled,
Or like a thief, which till death's doom be read,
Wisheth himself deliver'd from prison;
But damn'd and haled to execution,
Wisheth that still he might be imprisoned;
Yet grace, if thou repent, thou canst not lack;
But who shall give thee that grace to begin?
O, make thyself with holy mourning black,
And red with blushing, as thou art with sin;
Or wash thee in Christ's blood, which hath this might
That being red, it dyes red souls to white.

Holy Sonnet V

Here, Donne continues in confession. He does not ask not to be a passionate person, but that his passion might burn towards the greatest goal.

I am a little world made cunningly
Of elements, and an angelic spright,
But black sin hath betrayed to endless night
My worlds both parts, and oh! both parts must die.
You, which beyond that heaven which was most high
Have found new spheres and of new lands can write,
Pour new seas in mine eyes, that so I might
Drown my world with my weeping earnestly,
Or wash it, if it must be drowned no more:
But oh! it must be burnt; alas the fire
Of lust and envy burnt it heretofore,
And made it fouler; Let their flames retire,
And burn me, O Lord, with a fiery zeal
Of thee and thy house, which doth in eating heal.

Holy Sonnet VI

Read this one carefully; it is a poem of hope in grace. Donne is reaching bottom (these sonnets taken as a progression) and turning back up.

This is my play's last scene; here heavens appoint
My pilgrimage's last mile; and my race
Idly, yet quickly run, hath this last pace,
My span's last inch, my minute's latest point,
And gluttonous Death will instantly unjoint
My body and soul, and I shall sleep a space,
But my ever-waking part shall see that face,
Whose fear already shakes my every joint:
Then, as my soul to heaven her first seat takes flight,
And earth-born body in the earth shall dwell,
So fall my sins, that all may have their right,
To where they're bred and would press me to hell.
Impute me righteous, thus purged of evil,
For thus I leave the world, the flesh, the devil.

Holy Sonnet VII

In its early lines, this one seems it would have been better if we had set it into Eastertide. And note that the souls go to find their bodies: the resurrection of the body (the previous sonnet, VI, was not, on a careful reading, proclaiming a dis-embodied eternity). But we come into a Lenten attitude soon enough, as the various means by which we meet our ends are listed, and again the effort to bring ourselves to take our need for forgiveness seriously. Then a bit of wit snuck in, even here: the last line and a half remind us that though repenting and taking our need for forgiveness seriously is right and good — indeed, simply living in reality — the greater truth that releases and brings hope is that though we will never get all the way there, God has done something else, qualitatively different, to assure our hope.

At the round earth's imagined corners, blow
Your trumpets, angels, and arise, arise
From death, you numberless infinities
Of souls, and to your scattered bodies go,
All whom the flood did, and fire shall, o'erthrow,
All whom war, dearth, age, agues, tyrannies,
Despair, law, chance, hath slain, and you whose eyes,
Shall behold God, and never taste death's woe,
But let them sleep, Lord, and me mourn a space,
For, if above all these, my sins abound,
'Tis late to ask abundance of thy grace,
When we are there. Here on this lowly ground,
Teach me how to repent; for that's as good
As if thou'hadst seal'd my pardon with thy blood.

Holy Sonnet VIII

I take the first lines of this to be about Donne's father, who died when Donne was only four. Some argue he is referring to God the Father, but that does not sit easily with the reference to "soul" there. Others feel Donne leaves it purposefully ambiguous, which, of course, is very much possible, but the poem works best if it is simply Donne's father's soul, in heaven, free now, glorified in light, as angels are, and now equal to others — whereas as recusant Catholics his childhood family had been quite poor and socially on the outs. His father somehow has added to already full happiness the joy that Donne manages to escape hell's mouth ("valiantly"!), wide though the way is.

The perspective then moves to those in heaven, looking down on those living on earth: if those in heaven can see only what we here do and not into our minds and motives then what they see will likely, for various reasons, be less than impressive. A need for the self-reflection of a penitential season, indeed. But God has been working in us to bring us an impulse towards honesty about ourselves in the hopes that we will turn to him, for he knows us and all that is difficult, and put an ache in us to long to be unburdened.

If faithful souls be alike glorifi'd
As angels, then my father's soul doth see,
And adds this even to full felicity,
That valiantly I hell's wide mouth o'rstride:
But if our minds to these souls be descried
By circumstances, and by signs that be
Apparent in us not immediately,
How shall my mind's white truth by them be tried?
They see idolatrous lovers weep and mourn,
And stile blasphemous conjurers to call
On Jesu's name, and pharisaical
Dissemblers feign devotion. Then turn
O pensive soul, to God, for He knows best
Thy grief, for He put it into my breast.

Holy Sonnet IX

This one is a bit denser. The first lines raise complaints that we should be judged: so many other created things bring evil into the world and yet do not face the same standard as is expected of us. In other places, sermons for instance, Donne might venture a response to his own question; something about our distinction as created, yes, but in the *imago Dei*, the image of God. In sermons, he defends our ability to reason. Here he takes what we might call a blunter route: it is not ours to argue with God. But perhaps that is a set-up for line ten: the blood of Jesus is the only blood (blood is where the life is in Hebrew thought) of a human that is untainted and, thereby, worthy.

Donne then turns to poetic imagery: that his tears might cause heaven to forget: *Lethean*, deriving from the Greek word for forgetfulness or oblivion, and referencing the River Lethe, one of the four rivers of Hades in Classical mythology. If I understand it correctly, the spirits of the dead needed to drink from the river in order to forget their early lives — in a sense to have the record erased — to then be released into a new life.

In the top half of the poem, perhaps Donne is remembering the rather libertine period of his earlier years. Following immediately after Sonnet VIII, where he took us to his father's soul, in heaven, looking down on him and rejoicing at the hope his son has in God's grace, could Donne perhaps be hinting that the grief of the early loss of his father led him as a young man to a wild and reaching search for intimacy and the human connection he had lost? It is more than I can say beyond speculation, but, at any rate, here he hopes his tears of repentance will flow as a river leading God to forget, and he believes God's mercy will prevail.

If poisonous minerals, and if that tree,
Whose fruit threw death on else immortal us
If lecherous goats, if serpents envious
Cannot be damn'd, alas! why should I be
Why should intent or reason, born in me,
Make sins, else equal, in me more heinous
And, mercy being easy, and glorious
To God, in his stern wrath why threatens he?
But who am I, that dare dispute with thee?
O God, O! of thine only worthy blood
And my tears, make a heavenly Lethean flood
And drown in it my sin's black memory;
That thou remember them, some claim as debt,
I think it mercy if thou wilt forget.

Devotion II.

POST ACTIO LÆSA.

The Strength and the function of the senses, and other faculties, change and fail.

We return to Donne's Devotions. In this second one he is reckoning with the reality that has so quickly beset him. Oh, such a devastating feeling, as he notes the disease winning over his body's strength!

And a humble reminder, as we return to these Devotions, that they are excerpted.

MEDITATION.

The heavens are not the less constant, because they move continually, because they move continually one and the same way. The earth is not the more constant, because it lies still continually, because continually it changes and melts in all the parts thereof. Man, who is the noblest part of the earth, melts so away, as if he were a statue, not of earth, but of snow. We see his own envy melts him, he grows lean with that; he will say, another's beauty melts him; but he feels that a fever doth not melt him like snow, but pour him out like lead, like iron, like brass melted in a furnace; it doth not only melt him, but calcine him, reduce him to atoms, and to ashes; not to water, but to lime.

And how quickly? Sooner than thou canst receive an answer, sooner than thou canst conceive the question; earth is the centre of my body, heaven is the centre of my soul; these two are the natural places of these two; but those go not to these two in an equal pace: my body falls down without pushing; my soul does not go up without pulling; ascension is my soul's pace and measure, but precipitation my body's. And even angels, whose home is heaven, and who are winged too, yet had a ladder to go to heaven by steps.

The sun which goes so many miles in a minute, the stars of the firmament which go so very many more, go not so fast as my body to the earth. In the same instant that I feel the first attempt of the disease, I feel the victory; in the twinkling of an eye I can scarce see; instantly the taste is insipid and fatuous; instantly the appetite is dull and desireless; instantly the knees are sinking and strengthless; and in an instant, sleep, which is the picture, the copy of death, is taken away, that the original, death itself, may succeed, and that so I might have death to the life.

EXPOSTULATION.

...therefore how little soever I be, as *God calls things that are not, as though they were*, I, who am as though I were not, may call upon God, and say, My God, my God, why comes thine anger so fast upon me? Why dost thou melt me, scatter me, pour me like water upon the ground so instantly? Thou stayedst for the first world, in Noah's time, one hundred and twenty years; thou stayedst for a rebellious generation in the wilderness forty years, wilt thou stay no minute for me? Wilt thou make thy process and thy decree, thy citation and thy judgment, but one act? Thy summons, thy battle, thy victory, thy triumph, all but one act; and lead me captive, nay, deliver me captive to death, as soon as thou declarest me to be enemy, and so cut me off even with the drawing of thy sword out of the scabbard, and for that question,... How long was he sick? leave no other answer, but that the hand of death pressed upon him from the first minute? My God, my God, thou wast not wont to come in whirlwinds, but in soft and gentle air. Thy first breath breathed a soul into me, and shall thy breath blow it out? Thy breath in the congregation, thy word in the church, breathes communion and consolation here, and consummation hereafter; shall thy breath in this chamber breathe dissolution and destruction, divorce and separation? Surely it is not thou, it is not thy hand.

PRAYER.

O my God, who madest thyself a light in a bush, in the midst of these brambles and thorns of a sharp sickness, appear unto me so that I may see thee, and know thee to be my God, applying thyself to me, even in these sharp and thorny passages. Do this, O Lord, for his sake, who was not the less the King of heaven for thy suffering him to be crowned with thorns in this world.

Devotion III.

DECUBITUS SEQUITUR TANDEM.

The patient takes his bed.

The irrepressible poet: for Donne, his sickbed is the figure of practicing lying in the grave, unable to continue to practice his resurrection by rising from the bed.

Donne also, in his Expostulation here, wonders whether, having spent so much time in bed rather freely in his younger life, might be paying some sort of due on that time. Here are the first and third (last) stanzas of his (I must say, delightfully cheeky) romantic poem from that earlier period of his life, The Sun Rising, in which he chides the Sun for presuming that his schedule over-rules the timeless joy Donne and his lover enjoy in their own little cosmos of a bed:

Busy old fool, unruly sun,
Why dost thou thus,
Through windows, and through curtains call on us?
Must to thy motions lovers' seasons run?
Saucy pedantic wretch, go chide
Late school boys and sour prentices,
Go tell court huntsmen that the king will ride,
Call country ants to harvest offices;
Love, all alike, no season knows nor clime,
Nor hours, days, months, which are the rags of time.

She's all states, and all princes, I,
Nothing else is.
Princes do but play us; compared to this,
All honor's mimic, all wealth alchemy;
Thou, sun, art half as happy as we,
In that the world's contracted thus.
Thine age asks ease, and since thy duties be
To warm the world, that's done in warming us.
Shine here to us, and thou art everywhere;
This bed thy center is, these walls, thy sphere.

In his Expostulation Donne will here, as he was wont to do, cross over into a stringent theology of God's wrath directly causing of illness or suffering as judgment for sin, but, equally as ever, he does not stay there. That is not the final word. The final word is the mercy, the passionate love, and, most especially, the blood of God in Jesus. Also, in his Prayer he recognizes that he had often left God behind when he had climbed into a bed with a lover. He desires to turn all of this, intentionally, towards his renewal.

MEDITATION.

...here I am mine own ghost, and rather affright my beholders than instruct them; they conceive the worst of me now, and yet fear worse; they give me for dead now, and yet wonder how I do when they wake at midnight, and ask how I do to-morrow. Miserable, and (though common to all) inhuman posture, where I must practise my lying in the grave by lying still, and not practise my resurrection by rising any more.

EXPOSTULATION.

My God and my Jesus, my Lord and my Christ, my strength and my salvation, I hear thee, and I hearken to thee, when thou rebukest thy disciples, for rebuking them who brought children to thee; *Suffer little children to come to me*, sayest thou. Is there a verier child than I am now? I cannot say, with thy servant Jeremiah, *Lord, I am a child, and cannot speak*; but, O Lord, I am a sucking child, and cannot eat; a creeping child, and cannot go; how shall I come to thee? Whither shall I come to thee? To this bed? I have this weak and childish frowardness too, I cannot sit up, and yet am loth to go to bed. Shall I find thee in bed? Oh, have I always done so? The bed is not ordinarily thy scene, thy climate: Lord, dost thou not accuse me, dost thou not reproach to me my former sins, when thou layest me upon this bed? Is not this to hang a man at his own door, to lay him sick in his own bed of wantonness?...

As yet God suspends me between heaven and earth, as a meteor; and I am not in heaven because an earthly body clogs me, and I am not in the earth because a heavenly soul sustains me. And it is thine own law, O God, that *if a man be smitten so by another, as that he keep his bed, though he die not, he that hurt him must take care of his healing, and recompense him.*

Thy hand strikes me into this bed; and therefore, if I rise again, thou wilt be my recompense all the days of my life, in making the memory of this sickness beneficial to me; and if my body fall yet lower, thou wilt take my soul out of this bath, and present it to thy Father, washed again, and again, and again, in thine own tears, in thine own sweat, in thine own blood.

PRAYER.

Forget my bed, O Lord, as it hath been a bed of sloth, and worse than sloth; take me not, O Lord, at this advantage, to terrify my soul with saying, Now I have met thee there where thou hast so often departed from me; but having burnt up that bed by these vehement heats, and washed that bed in these abundant sweats, make my bed again, O Lord, and enable me, according to thy command, *to commune with mine own heart upon my bed, and be still*; to provide a bed for all my former sins whilst I lie upon this bed, and a grave for my sins before I come to my grave; and when I have deposited them in the wounds of thy Son, to rest in that assurance, that my conscience is discharged from further anxiety, and my soul from further danger, and my memory from further calumny. Do this, O Lord, for his sake, who did and suffered so much, that thou mightest, as well in thy justice as in thy mercy, do it for me, thy Son, our Saviour, Christ Jesus.

Devotion IV.

MEDICUSQUE VOCATUR.

The physician is sent for.

I find a juxtaposition here fascinating: Donne so often has the idea that his sufferings are in direct judgment from God for his sins, but also, here especially, we see the profoundly high esteem in which he holds the human. We may feel this to be an oxymoron; Donne considered it a congruency.

MEDITATION.

It is too little to call man a little world; except God, man is a diminutive to nothing. Man consists of more pieces, more parts, than the world; than the world doth, nay, than the world is. And if those pieces were extended, and stretched out in man as they are in the world, man would be the giant, and the world the dwarf; the world but the map, and the man the world. If all the veins in our bodies were extended to rivers, and all the sinews to veins of mines, and all the muscles that lie upon one another, to hills, and all the bones to quarries of stones, and all the other pieces to the proportion of those which correspond to them in the world, the air would be too little for this orb of man to move in, the firmament would be but enough for this star; for, as the whole world hath nothing, to which something in man doth not answer, so hath man many pieces of which the whole world hath no representation.

Enlarge this meditation upon this great world, man, so far as to consider the immensity of the creatures this world produces; our creatures are our thoughts, creatures that are born giants; that reach from east to west, from earth to heaven; that do not only bestride all the sea and land, but span the sun and firmament at once; my thoughts reach all, comprehend all. Inexplicable mystery; I their creator am in a close prison, in a sick bed, any where, and any one of my creatures, my thoughts, is with the sun, and beyond the sun, overtakes the sun, and overgoes the sun in one pace, one step, everywhere...

O miserable abundance, O beggarly riches! how much do we lack of having remedies for every disease, when as yet we have not names for them? But we have a Hercules against these giants, these monsters; that is, the physician; he musters up all the forces of the other world to succour this, all nature to relieve man. We have the physician, but we are not the physician. Here we shrink in our proportion, sink in our dignity, in respect of very mean creatures, who are physicians to themselves...

Call back therefore thy meditation again, and bring it down: what's become of man's great extent and proportion, when himself shrinks himself and consumes himself to a handful of dust; what's become of his soaring thoughts, his compassing thoughts, when himself brings himself to the ignorance, to the thoughtlessness, of the grave? His diseases are his own, but the physician is not; he hath them at home, but he must send for the physician.

PRAYER.

O most mighty and most merciful God, who art so the God of health and strength, as that without thee all health is but the fuel, and all strength but the bellows of sin; behold me under the vehemence of two diseases, and under the necessity of two physicians, authorized by thee, the bodily, and the spiritual physician. I come to both as to thine ordinance, and bless and glorify thy name that, in both cases, thou hast afforded help to man by the ministry of man. Even in the new Jerusalem, in heaven itself, it hath pleased thee to discover a tree, which is *a tree of life there, but the leaves thereof are for the healing of the nations.* Life itself is with thee there, for thou art life; and all kinds of health, wrought upon us here by thine instruments, descend from thence. *Thou wouldst have healed Babylon, but she is not healed.* Take from me, O Lord, her perverseness, her wilfulness, her refractoriness, and hear thy Spirit saying in my soul: Heal me, O Lord, for I would be healed.

Devotion XVII.

NUNC LENTO SONITU DICUNT, MORIERIS.

Now, this bell tolling softly for another, says to me: Thou must die.

This Devotion, XVII, is the setting for the lines that emerged to fame: "No man is an island, entire of himself;" and "...never send to know for whom the bell tolls; it tolls for thee." These were not abstract philosophizing by Donne. Instead, one gets the sense that he has gained some reflective space, made approach to peace with the possibility of his death through this illness. The last line, at least, suggests something to that effect.

MEDITATION.

Perchance he for whom this bell tolls may be so ill, as that he knows not it tolls for him; and perchance I may think myself so much better than I am, as that they who are about me, and see my state, may have caused it to toll for me, and I know not that.

The church is Catholic, universal, so are all her actions; all that she does belongs to all. When she baptizes a child, that action concerns me; for that child is thereby connected to that body which is my head too, and ingrafted into that body whereof I am a member. And when she buries a man, that action concerns me: all mankind is of one author, and is one volume; when one man dies, one chapter is not torn out of the book, but translated into a better language; and every chapter must be so translated; God employs several translators; some pieces are translated by age, some by sickness, some by war, some by justice; but God's hand is in every translation, and his hand shall bind up all our scattered leaves again for that library where every book shall lie open to one another.

As therefore the bell that rings to a sermon calls not upon the preacher only, but upon the congregation to come, so this bell calls us all; but how much more me, who am brought so near the door by this sickness...

Who casts not up his eye to the sun when it rises? but who takes off his eye from a comet when that breaks out? Who bends not his ear to any bell which upon any occasion rings? but who can remove it from that bell which is passing a piece of himself out of this world? No man is an island, entire of itself; every man is a piece of the continent, a part of the main. If a clod be washed away by the sea, Europe is the less, as well as if a promontory were, as well as if a manor of thy friend's or of thine own were: any man's death diminishes me, because I am involved in mankind, and therefore never send to know for whom the bells tolls; it tolls for thee.

Neither can we call this a begging of misery, or a borrowing of misery, as though we were not miserable enough of ourselves, but must fetch in more from the next house, in taking upon us the misery of our neighbours. Truly it were an excusable covetousness if we did, for affliction is a treasure, and scarce any man hath enough of it. No man hath affliction enough that is not matured and ripened by it, and made fit for God by that affliction. If a man carry treasure in bullion, or in a wedge of gold, and have none coined into current money, his treasure will not defray him as he travels. Tribulation is treasure in the nature of it, but it is not current money in the use of it, except we get nearer and nearer our home, heaven, by it.

Another man may be sick too, and sick to death, and this affliction may lie in his bowels, as gold in a mine, and be of no use to him; but this bell, that tells me of his affliction, digs out and applies that gold to me: if by this consideration of another's danger I take mine own into contemplation, and so secure myself, by making my recourse to my God, who is our only security.

PRAYER.

When thy Son cried out upon the cross, *My God, my God, why hast thou forsaken me?* he spake not so much in his own person, as in the person of the church, and of his afflicted members, who in deep distresses might fear thy forsaking. This patient, O most blessed God, is one of them; in his behalf, and in his name, hear thy Son crying to thee, *My God, my God, why hast thou forsaken me?* and forsake him not; but with thy left hand lay his body in the grave (if that be thy determination upon him), and with thy right hand receive his soul into thy kingdom, and unite him and us in one communion of saints. Amen.

A Hymn to God the Father

This confessional poem of Donne's is believed to have been written after his sudden and severe illness that occasioned his Devotions. It was set to music by a later contemporary, John Hilton, who was born about twenty-five years after Donne, and whose life overlapped Donne's for three decades. It is often sung during Lent in Anglican churches; harmony having been added in the early twentieth century by two composers.

It is a fairly straightforward piece, and ranges from original sin, shared by all humans, through to habitual sins that are so difficult to shed (once we have taught our bodies or brains that pleasure or relief is there), through to ultimate or existential fear. But, again, Donne happily relies in the end on the accomplished and finished work of Jesus, and his fears are alleviated.

However, of course, it is not all that straightforward. There are two puns here as well:

Donne is punned through *done*. And one other, less obvious: Donne's wife's name was Anne *More*. We recall that Donne's father died when Donne was a tender four, and his family being recusant Catholics, Donne's start in life was not easy. However, by age twenty-five he was on his way to a diplomatic career, his brilliance showing through, and had an advocate in Sir Thomas Edgerton, at whose home in London (and close to Whitehall) Donne lived — right in the center of the all-important social scene. Ah. But over the next few years Donne fell in love with Egerton's niece, Anne More. Not being able to secure either Egerton's or Anne's father's blessing, they married secretly late in 1601. Anne's father, George, was Lieutenant of the Tower. These were not people to be trifled with.

Donne ended up dismissed from his role and thrown into prison, along with the priest who married them. (A warning to me and all priests to take weddings seriously!) Once the marriage was demonstrated to be valid Donne was released, and he managed to have the priest released as well. But when it all went down Donne wrote to Anne to tell her he had lost his post — their livelihood and his dreams for a future — and signed the letter, *John Donne, Anne Donne, Un-done*. Even in this, unable to resist a play on words.

It did not make for an easy life for his wife. All he could put together was a country life in a small house far from the opportunities of town and owned by Anne's cousin who, presumably, had mercy on them. A few years later they moved house, but again to tight quarters in the country. In the meantime, Anne birthed a baby nearly annually. Eventually, in 1609, he was reconciled to his father-in-law, and his wife's dowry was granted. Donne's ordination followed a handful of years later, and his future brightened again.

But perhaps later in life — he fell ill in 1623, Anne had died in 1617, so if this was written after his illness then it was a good bit later than all those fireworks, and after he had wildly succeeded as a preacher and been set in the best role the Church of England had, as Dean of St Paul's, London — but still, perhaps later in life he reflected and felt guilt for all he had dragged Anne through. Surely his grieving at her death testified that he deeply loved her.

Wilt thou forgive that sin where I begun,
Which was my sin, though it were done before?
Wilt thou forgive that sin, through which I run,
And do run still, though still I do deplore?
When thou hast done, thou hast not done,
For I have more.

Wilt thou forgive that sin which I have won
Others to sin, and made my sin their door?
Wilt thou forgive that sin which I did shun
A year or two, but wallow'd in, a score?
When thou hast done, thou hast not done,
For I have more.

I have a sin of fear, that when I have spun
My last thread, I shall perish on the shore;
But swear by thyself, that at my death thy Son
Shall shine as he shines now, and heretofore;
And, having done that, thou hast done;
I fear no more.

SERMONS

If John Donne was the master of wit how did that affect his sermons? What happens when a poet takes to the pulpit and speaks in a more direct, didactic genre? It might well be a disaster: impressionist, one might say, but lacking cohesion.

Donne was too brilliant and too pastorally caring for that. He managed the genre transition just fine, even in an era of sermons that lasted forty-five minutes to an hour or more, and therefore had quite a few points to develop and transitions to manage. But still, the poetic gift *does* shine through, and how. His poetic gifts – his genius for paradox and his profound depth of feeling and empathy – shine through without disintegrating the overall logical and propositional structure of the sermons.

In her recently-published biography of Donne, Katherine Rundell notes the paradox of the poet and the logically-structured preacher, in one: "To read the full text of a Donne sermon is a little like mounting a horse only to discover that it is an elephant..."[5]

Yet, at the same time, she notes that his sermons followed a common rhetorical structure of the day – common structure, uncommon preacher:

> Renaissance sermons were long: often upwards of an hour [O, happy era!]...
> For all their length, his sermons were never sombre or staid: there were passionate performances, attempts to strike a match against the rough walls of the listener's chest cavities... Donne unleashed his charisma, for the first time, upon live, reactive audiences who could eat it in full and demand more..."[6]

Evelyn Simpson, who with a colleague produced a highly-respected ten-volume set of Donne's sermons midway through the twentieth century (considered by many the definitive collection), began her introduction to a summary volume of his sermons, "DONNE's sermons are admittedly unique. Charles Eliot Norton wrote of them, 'They are as unlike any other sermons as his poems are unlike any other poetry.'" It is difficult to imagine Donne did not smile from heaven above at that. Simpson

---

[5] *Ibid., 254.*
[6] *Ibid.,* 222 & 224.

continues, "Coleridge was deeply interested in them and wrote profuse annotations in the margins of the 1640 folio of Donne's *LXXX Sermons.*"[7] T. S. Eliot, was, apparently, less impressed. He derived his probably-most-beloved poem rather significantly from the preacher he backed instead, Lancelot Andrewes. But, Simpson notes, "Donne has the advantage over Andrewes in that he was a poet who did not lose his poetical imagination when he entered the pulpit."[8] Indeed.

A memorable line from the introduction to the Oxford World's Classics volume on Donne: "The dependable solidity of the material world vanishes when Donne mounts the pulpit." [9] A rather delicious sentence, itself, and — even better — a delicious sentiment! The editor of the volume believes that "The theological interests that dominate Donne's sermons can be seen as

---

7. Evelyn Simpson (ed. And introduction), *John Donne's Sermons on the Psalms and Gospels* (University of California Press, 2003), 1. Regarding T.S. Eliot, I am referring to his The Journey of the Magi. See Lancelot Andrewe's sermon at Whitehall on Christmas Day 1622.

[8] *Ibid., 1.*

[9] John Carey (ed. and introduction), *John Donne, The Major Works, including Song and Sonnets and sermons* (Oxford World's Classics, Oxford University Press, 2000), xxxi.

reformulations of imaginings that occur in his poems", for example, "his wonderment at God's creation of the world out of nothing..." and "the belief that 'all that the soul does it does in, and with, and by the body.'"[10]

Latin was the language of the educated at that time, and hence it was commonplace to intersperse Latin phrases and terms (and occasionally Greek) into a sermon for emphasis, certainly in a venue like St Paul's. Sometimes Donne himself provided the English translation immediately after – using the ancient language for rhetorical effect but rescuing his audience. Given that he rescues us, his audience, I have left his rhetorical uses of the ancient languages intact. There are a few places where he does not translate it, seemingly because he judged the phrase or term to be commonplace enough, or the context to be clear enough, to allow the audience to sort it out. I have tended to leave those as he did. The spelling, on the other hand, I have almost always adapted to our day, perhaps occasionally missing one or just leaving one that seems fun.

Donne used italics quite liberally; it was tempting to keep these under the idea that, were the reader to imagine the sermon being spoken, then the

---

[10] *Ibid.*, xxx-xxxi.

emphasis provided by the italics would add depth and color. In the end, I decided there were just too many and they are likely a distraction and an impediment to reading. I have kept a few, here and there, where I sense the emphasis will come through more than distraction does. I have kept his italicizing of quotes of Scripture and also in those places where I kept his use of an ancient language and the following translation – when Donne himself italicized that. Donne also used capitalization quite liberally – for emphasis, not per any strict grammatical rule. Most of this I have also changed, but a bit of it — major theological ideas or events (the Cross) — has seemed good to keep, and gives a flavor of his style and times. Finally, I have sometimes taken the liberty of introducing paragraph breaks where he did not, his era not having their attention spans mercilessly assaulted day in and day out by sound bites and social media.

Donne was an Anglican, and arguably what we might call a vigorous example of his tradition's famous *via media*, or middle way, in that he held together both close sympathy for some Catholic beliefs – he had a rather high view of Mary, as we saw in Annunciation, for instance – and enthusiastically embraced the Reformation's renewed interest in going back *ad fontes*, to the sources, both the primary sources of the Scriptures themselves and also the early Fathers of the faith. Thus, in his sermons, we will find that Irenæus, Basil, and, perhaps most often, Epiphanius, along with others, pop up, as Donne parenthetically notes that they gave him this or that insight, or that they affirm what he is proclaiming.

Finally, where we take significant breaks in a sermon, I will attempt to give just enough editorial context between the excerpts to connect the basic dots. These will be demarcated by being italicized.

PREACHED IN LENT, TO THE KING.

April 20. 1630.

I find this sermon remarkable in many ways and therefore have included quite a long excerpt overall — more of it is here than not. This sermon is about the most difficult question of all: How we sort trusting God's goodness and power in a world where chaos and evil, suffering and grief abound?

Job is an enigmatic book, to say the least. I tell my parishioners when they seem befuddled by it that the first thing to notice is that it is there at all: no government in the world would allow the opening behind-the-scenes look at the Satan and God in conversation, if that were a top-secret conversation between them and a hostile power. As uncomfortable as the whole scene is, there it is, for everyone to see.

It is enigmatic in other ways as well: is it historical or parable? Possibly the oldest book in the canon of the Scriptures, or possibly later, a bit of a morality tale so to speak, during the days of the exile? And so many words that are unique to the Scriptures. And, forgive me for this, but no one knows for sure where Uz, well, was.

It is all deeply intriguing, to be sure. But, also, none of that is strictly our concern here: here we rejoice (solemnly perhaps, but still) at the courage (if I can put it that way), the determination, of our God to let us know that he knows — he knows our struggles, losses, griefs in this our weary and worn way of this world. He hears us; he is patient; he is near.

Donne was courageous enough to bring all of this forward basically four hundred years ago; and to feed it to his people, if you will, for their soul's sake. And so, we too venture along this enigmatic and sometimes ominous path as we continue our pilgrimage.

JOB 16.17, 18, 19. NOT FOR ANY INJUSTICE IN MY HANDS: ALSO MY PRAYER IS PURE. O EARTH COVER NOT THOU MY BLOOD; AND LET MY CRY HAVE NO PLACE. ALSO NOW BEHOLD, MY WITNESSE IS IN HEAVEN, AND MY RECORD IS ON HIGH.

Job's friends (as, in civility we are faine to call them, because they came upon a civil pretence, to visit him, and to comfort him) had now done speaking. It was long before they would have done. *Audivi frequenter talia,* says Job to them, I have often heard such things as you say, they are not new to me; and therefore, *Onerosi consolatores,* miserable comforters, troublesome comforters are ye all, old and new. But, *Numquid finem habebunt verba ventosa,* saies he, shall your windy words, your empty, your aery, your frothy words have any end? Now they have an end. Eliphas ends his charge in the last, and in this chapter Job begins to answer for himself. But how? By a middle way. Job does not justify himself; but yet he does not prevaricate, he does not betray his Innocence neither. For there may be a pusillanimity even towards God; A man may over-clog his own conscience, and belie himself in his confessions, out of a distempered jealousy, and suspicion of God's purposes upon him; Job does not so.

Job begins to answer, but "by a middle way." Already we see the worth, if you will, of the book of Job. It raises life's toughest question and refuses to hide in pat answers. And it has always been a challenge: is it historical or essentially a parable? Is it possibly the oldest of the books of the Bible or written in a middle stage of ancient Israel's kingdom? These are still-living controversies. And how are Job's sufferings to be understood? I love Donne's honesty. As he continues he faces up to how challenging this book has always been to those who strive to interpret it. One of the great things about reading Donne is that he introduces us to the early Fathers of the church: ad fontes *was a rallying cry of the Reformation: "to the fountains!", meaning the ancient sources of wisdom, closest to the life of Christ. But here Donne is forced to move a few generations out.*

Many men have troubled themselves more, how the soul comes into man, then how it goes out; They wrangle, whether it comes in by Infusion from God, or by Propagation from parents, and never consider, whether it shall return to Him that made it, or to him that marr'd it, to Him that gave it, or to him that corrupted it. So, many of our Expositors upon this Book of Job, have spent themselves upon the Person, and the Place, and the Time, who Job was, when Job was, where Job was, and whether there were ever any such person as Job, or no; and have passed over too slightly the senses, and doctrines of the Book. St. Gregory hath, (to good use) given us many morals, (as he calls them) upon this Book, but, truly, not many Literals, for, for the most part, he bends all the sufferings of Job figuratively, mystically upon Christ. Origen, who (except St. Gregory) hath written most of this Book, and yet gone but a little way into the book neither, doth never pretend much literalness in his expositions, so that we are not to look for that at Origen's hands. We must not therefore refuse the assistance of later men, in the exposition of this text, *Not for any Injustice in my hands, &c.*

So, having cleared that out of the way, Donne finds his rhythm. Perhaps it is worth remembering here that Donne knew quite a lot – too much, really – loss and heavy grief himself. He must have read Job with a sympathetic heart and curious soul. As Donne continues, he will first go courageously straight to how this book faces up to life's toughest realities.

In this Chapter, and before this text, we have Job's anatomy, Job's skeleton, the ruins to which he was reduced. In the eighth verse he takes knowledge, that God had filled him with leanness and wrinkles, and that those wrinkles, and that leanness were witnesses against him, and, that they that hated him, had torn him in pieces, in the ninth verse. In the eleventh verse, that God had delivered him over to the ungodly, and, that God himself had shaken him in pieces, and set him up as a mark to shoot at, in the twelfth verse; that God had cleft his reins, and poured out his gall upon the ground, in the thirteenth verse, and in the fourteenth, that he broke him, breach after breach, and run over him as a giant, and at last, in the sixteenth verse, that foulness was upon his face, and the shadow of death upon his eyelids. Now, let me ask in Job's behalf God's question to Ezekiel, *Putasne vivent ossa ista?* Doest thou believe that these bones can live? Can this anatomy, this skeleton, these ruin, this rubbage of Job speak? It can, it does in this text, *Not for any injustice in my hands, &c.*

And, in these words, it delivers us, first, the confidence of a godly man; do God what he will, say ye what ye will, that because I am more afflicted than other men, therefore I am guilty of more heinous sins then other men, yet I know, that whatsoever God's end be in this proceeding, it is not for any injustice in my hands, Also my prayer is pure. Secondly, it delivers us that kind of infirm anguish, and indignation, that half-distemper, that expostulation with God, which sometimes comes to an excess even in good and godly men, *O earth cover not thou my blood, and let my cry have no place;* I desire not that any thing should be concealed or disguised, let all that ever I have done be written in my forehead, and read by all men. And then thirdly and lastly, it delivers us the foundation of his confidence, and the recovery from this his infirmity, and from his excess in the manner of expressing it, if he have been over-bold therein, *My witness is in heaven, and my record is on high;* God is his witness, that that which they charge him with, is false, that that which he says in his own discharge (in that sense that he says it) is true; and in these three, Job's protestation, not guilty, Job's manifest, I would all the world knew all, Job's establishment, and consolidation, *my witness is in heaven;* in these three branches, and in some fruits, which, in passing, we shall gather from them, we shall determine all that appertains to these words.

As a preacher myself, how I envy Donne's courage! He will disclaim that on this day he will be giving them nothing special (relative to his rather high standard), and he hopes they can tolerate it. But also, clever rhetoric!, he is inducing a touch of sympathetic relaxation in their defenses before he calls upon them (us) to notice their (our) own similarity to the friends of Job – and goodness that's clever of him, because who wants to hear that straight? But Donne will call to us to notice that we often have the same attitude, and to change and to show mercy and grace. And in that, we might note that Donne, the Anglican – he of the "middle way" – notes how easily one that is conscientious in his day was presumed "Puritan," and one who loved the ancient ways and worship of the church was presumed "Papist." His audience got the point: both conscientiousness and the ancient forms of worship have their place, and the two both fit, in the right measure and degree, in the Anglican way.

I remember S. Gregory, in handling one text, professes, that he will endeavor to handle it so, *Vt ejus altitudo non sic fieret nescientibus cognita, ut esset scientibus onerosa;* so, as that the weakest understanding might comprehend the highest points, and the highest understanding not be weary to hear ordinary doctrines so delivered. Indeed it is a good art, to deliver deep points in a holy plainness, and plain points in a holy delightfulness: for, many times, one part of our auditory understands us not, when we have done, and so they are weary; and another part understands us before we begun, and so they are weary. Today my humble petition must be, that you will be content to hear plain things plainly delivered. Of which, be this the first, that Job found himself under the oppression, and calumny of that misinterpretation, that kings themselves, and states, and churches have not escaped. The tower of Siloam fell and slew them, therefore they were the greater sinners in Jerusalem; this man prospers not in the world, therefore he proceeds not in the fear of God; the heir wastes the estate, therefore the estate was ill gotten, are hasty conclusions in private affaires. Treasures are empty, therefore there are unnecessary wastes; discontented persons murmur, therefore things are ill-carried; our neighbors' prosper by action, therefore we perish by not appearing, are hasty conclusions in state affairs. This man is affected when he hears a blasphemous oath; and when he looks upon the general liberty of sinning, therefore he is a Puritan; that man loves the ancient forms, and doctrines, and disciplines of the church, and retains, and delights in the reverend names of priest, and altar, and sacrifice, therefore he is a Papist, are hasty conclusions in church affairs. When we do fall under these misinterpretations, and ill applications of God's proceedings, we may say with Job, I also could speak, as you do; if your soul were in my soul's stead, I could heap up words against you, and shake my head at you, conclude desperately, speak scornfully of you. But I will not; yet I will not betray myself, I will make my protestation, what end soever God propose to himself in this his proceeding, *It is not for any injustice in my hands, also my prayer is pure.*

In these two, cleanness of hands, pureness of prayer, are all religious duties comprehended: for clean hands denote justice and righteousness towards men, and pure prayer devotion, and the service and worship of God. Job protests for both. Therefore does Origen say of Job, *Certè puto, quod & audio dicere,* I do verily believe, and therefore may be bold to say, that for constancy and fidelity towards God, Job did exceed, *Non soum homines, sed & ipsos Angelos,* not only men, but angels themselves; for, says Origen, Job did not only suffer, *Absque culpa,* without being guilty of those things to which his afflictions were imputed, but he suffered with giving of thanks, he said grace when he had no meat, when God gave him stones for bread, and scorpions for fish; he praised God as much for the affliction itself, as for his former, or his subsequent benefits and blessings. Not that Job was merely innocent, but that he was guilty of no such things, as might confer those conclusions, which, from his afflictions, his enemies raised. If I justify myself, says Job, mine own mouth shall condemn me; every self-justification is a self-condemnation; when I give judgment for myself, I am therein a witness against myself. If I say I am perfect, says he in the same place, even that proves me perverse; if I say I never go out of the way, I am out then, and therefore because I say so: I have sinned, says he, what shall I do unto thee O thou preserver of men? Job felt the hand of destruction upon him, and he felt the hand of preservation too; and it was all one hand; this is God's method, and his alone, to preserve by destroying. Men of this world do sometimes repair, and recompense those men whom they have oppressed before, but this is an after recompense; God's first intention even when he destroys is to preserve, as a physician's first intention, in the most distasteful physic, is health; even God's demolitions are super-edifications, his anatomies, his dissections are so many re-compactings, so many resurrections; God winds us off the skein, that he may weave us up into the whole piece, and he cuts us out of the whole piece into pieces, that he may make us up into a whole garment.

Alas, Lent is for strong medicine, and strong medicine is what Donne has just been preaching. But, he has said, strong medicine is, still, medicine, and administered in love and hope. So now, having given us quite a dose, Donne will begin to turn, and to try to show us the way to the inner peace and confidence that remained at Job's core, despite all.

But for all these humiliations, and confessions, Job doth not waive his protestation: my righteousness I hold fast, and my heart shall not reproach me as long as I live. Not that I shall never sin, but never leave any sin unrepented; and then, my heart cannot reproach me of a repented sin, without reproaching God himself. The sun must not set upon my anger; much less will I let the sun set upon the anger of God towards me, or sleep in an unrepented sin. Every night's sleep is a *Nunc dimittis*; then the Lord lets his servant depart in peace. Thy lying down is a valediction, a parting, a taking leave, (shall I say so?) a shaking hands with God; and, when thou shakest hands with God, let those hands be clean. Enter into thy grave, thy metaphorical, thy quotidian grave, thy bed, as thou enteredest into the church at first, by water, by baptism; rebaptize thyself every night, in Job's snow water, in holy tears that may cool the inordinate lusts of thy heart...

Sleep with clean hands, either kept clean all day, by integrity; or washed clean, at night, by repentance; and whensoever thou wakest, though all Job's messengers thunder about thee, and all Job's friends multiply misinterpretations against thee, yet Job's protestation shall be thy protestation, what end soever God have in this proceeding, *It is not for any injustice in my hands,* and the other part of his protestation too, *also my prayer is pure.*

Often times in these sermons, when Donne gets into the middle he goes on an excursus or two. Happy days, those when preachers could go for an hour or so. These excurses are the bits I tend to skip over when introducing people to this magnificent preacher's works. But here he works his way up to one that, granted while still an excursus, I have felt worthy of keeping. Donne will do a little bit of transition to defend Collects: written prayers of gathered wisdom which are meant to guide us and to speak for us, gathering our hearts to the hearts of others who have called and do call upon the name of the Lord Jesus: "collecting" that wisdom to "collect" our hearts together in one voice. Or "collecting" the lessons of the Eucharistic liturgy for that week into one synthesized theological point.

Controversy as to whether such a prayer could be genuine lived in Donne's day as well. Alas. But Donne will take it one step further: he will dare to argue that the Collect is the prayer that is most truly mine, *personally. To be fair, perhaps he overdoes it a bit to my taste; I imagine he was pushed to that by the controversy in his own times, as the Puritans rose in strength and the currents that would later lead to the English Civil War began to flow with more power.*

As clean hands denote all righteousness towards man, so do pure prayers all devotion, and worship, and service of God. For, we are of the household of the faithful, and the service which we are to do, as his household servants, is prayer; for, his house is the house of prayer. And therein only is it possible to us, to fulfil that commandment, pray continually, that continually, in all our familiar actions, we may serve God, glorify God, (whether we eat or drink, we may do it to his glory) and every glorifying, every thanksgiving, is prayer; there cannot be a more effectual prayer for future, than a thankful acknowledgment of former benefits. *Petite, & dabitur;* how often is that repeated in the Gospel, and in the Epistles? Ask, and it shall be given you; no grant without prayer, no denial upon prayer.

It must he prayer, and my prayer; *also my prayer is pure*... It must be mine own prayer, and no prayer is so truly, or so properly mine, as that that the church hath delivered and recommended to me. In sudden and unpremeditate prayer, I am not always I; and when I am not myself, my prayer is not my prayer. Passions and affections sometimes, sometimes bodily infirmities, and sometimes a vain desire of being eloquent in prayer, aliens me, withdraws me from myself, and then that prayer is not my prayer...

In that African council, in which St. Augustine was present, to remedy the abuse of various forms of prayers, which divers churches assumed, it was decreed that no prayers should be received in the church, but such as were composed, or approved by the council. We have proceeded so too; no prayers received for public use, but those that are delivered by public authority; and so, they become my prayers. As the law of the land is my law, and I have an inheritance in it, so the prayers of the church are my prayers, and I have an interest in them, because I am a son of that family. My baptism is mine, and my absolution is mine, because the church hath given them to me, and so are her prayers mine. You would scarce thank a man for an extemporal elegy, or epigram, or panegyric in your praise, if it cost the poet, or the orator no pains. God will scarce hearken to sudden, inconsidered, irreverent prayers. Men will study even for compliments; and princes and ambassadors will not speak to one another, without thinking what they will say. Let not us put God to speak to us so, (preaching is God's speaking to us) let not us speak to God so, (praying is our speaking to God) not extemporally, unadvisedly, inconsiderately. Prayer must be my prayer; and even in this kind, what have I that I have not received? I have received my prayer altogether, as a bundle of myrrh, in that prayer which I have received from my Saviour, and then I have received it appropriated to me, and apportioned to my particular necessities, and sacrifices, by the piety and wisdom of the church; so it is my prayer, and, as Job's prayer was, pure prayer, also my prayer is pure.

The Holy Ghost hath so marshalled and disposed the qualifications of prayer in this place, as that there is no pure prayer without clean hands. The lifting up of hands was the gesture of prayer, even among the heathen, *Manibus supplex orare supinis*. Amongst the Jews, Prayer, and the lifting up of hands, was one and the same thing, Let the lifting up of my hands be an evening sacrifice; and, longer than Moses' hands were lifted up, his prayer had no effect. All this, perchance therefore especially, that this lifting up of my hands, brings them into my sight; then I can see them, and see whether they be clean, or no, and consider, that if I see impurity in my hands, God sees impurity in my prayer. Can I think to receive ease from God with that hand that oppresses another? Mercy from God with that hand that exercises cruelty upon another? Or bounty from God with that hand that withholds right from another? Prayer is our hand, but it must be a clean hand, pure prayer.

And now Donne begins to swing back to the main topic, acknowledging that this has been an excursus, or, as the poet puts it in an image, a "branch." As he does so, notice another difficulty which also, sadly, apparently infected his times as well – "health and wealth" prayers, or prayers in mean spirit for ill against others.

...To end this branch, let not thy prayer be lucrative, nor vindictive, pray not for temporal superfluities, pray not for the confusion of them that differ from thee in opinion, or in manners, but condition thy prayer, inanimate thy prayer with the glory of God, and thine own everlasting happiness, and the edification of others, and this prayer is Job's prayer, pure prayer. And farther we enlarge not his protestation, *My hands are clean,* I do no man wrong, my prayer is pure, I mock not God. But because continuing under so great afflictions, men would not believe this, he proceeds, perchance to some excess, and inconsiderateness, in desiring a manifestation of all his actions, *O earth, cover not thou my blood, and let my cry have no place.*

Again, we will see this book of Job, in facing life's toughest realities, pushes us to the limits and gets behind our defenses. Donne will now ask what Job means by calling on the earth not to cover his blood. Donne walks through some of the options wise teachers from the past have offered: St. Gregory argued that because Job is a type of Christ then he longed for something that most men would fear – that all that he had ever done or declared be made known to all the world, in the manner that the life and sufferings of Christ are proclaimed. Donne says this is good in and of itself, but that it does not truly fit the context.

Then Donne notes that Cajetan, following Rabbi Aben Ezra, argued that Job is afraid lest the earth not conspire in his suffering, to deny him burial and that he not be forsaken by God in his death. This, too,

Donne says, has its good use, but cannot measure up to "the sense of this phrase, of this elegancy, this vehemency of the Holy Ghost..."

And then Donne notes that to his knowledge St. John Chrysostom was the first to give what he considered a better interpretation: that those who have suffered beyond what they deserve long that people know the whole story, so that they may then be vindicated in the eyes of the watching and judging world. And, in that direction, that blood here has at least significantly a figurative meaning, a spiritual meaning: blood as the life of the soul. We return to Donne as he goes forward with this.

This then being thus established, that blood in this text, is the blood of the soul, exhausted by sin, (for every sin is an incision of the soul, a lancination, a phlebotomy, a letting of the soul blood, and then a delight in sin, is a going with open veins into a warm bath, and bleeding to death) this will be the force of Job's admiration, or imprecation, O earth cover not thou my blood, I am content to stand as naked now, as I shall do at the day of judgment, when all men shall see all men's actions, I desire no disguise, I deny, I excuse, I extenuate nothing that ever I did, I would mine enemies knew my worst, that they might study some other reason of God's thus proceeding with me, than those heinous sins...

But had Job been able to have stood out this trial? Was Job so innocent, as that he need not care, though all the world knew all? Perchance there may have been some excess, some inordinateness in his manner of his expressing it... We cannot say, that there was no excess in Moses' *Dele me*, pardon this people, or blot my name out of thy book; or that there was no excess in St. Paul's *Anathema pro fratribus*, that he wished to be accursed, to be separated from Christ for his brethren. But for Job, we shall not need this excuse; for, either we may restrain his words to those sins, which they imputed to him, and then they have but the nature of that protestation, which David made so often to God, *Judge me, O Lord, according to my righteousness, according to mine innocency, according to the cleanness of my hands*; which was not spoken by David simply, but respectively, not of all his sins, but of those which Saul pursued him for: Or, if we enlarge Job's words generally to all his sins, we must consider them to be spoken after his repentance, and reconciliation to God thereupon; if they knew, (may Job have said) how it stood between God and my soul, how earnestly I have repented, how fully he hath forgiven, they would never say, these afflictions proceeded from those sins.

Some of this, I suspect, have been slow going; it has been for me. The language and expression differences are thick throughout this part of the sermon. But persevere in it a bit farther, and there is a major Gospel payoff. In this next paragraph, Donne will argue that if not only his sins were known but also the vast expense of the opportunity cost to his well-being, his joy, energy, hope – his vision of an open and happy horizon, one might say – then people would also see the depth of his confessions and the willingness of God to forgive and to show mercy. And be sure not to miss the switching of referent regarding blood.

And truly, so may I, so may every soul say, that is rectified, refreshed, restored, re-established by the seals of God's pardon, and his mercy, so the world would take knowledge of the consequences of my sins, as well as of the sins themselves, and read my leaves on both sides, and hear the second part of my story, as well as the first; so the world would look upon my temporal calamities, the bodily sicknesses, and the penuriousness of my fortune contracted by my sins, and upon my spiritual calamities, dejections of spirit, sadness of heart, declinations towards a diffidence and distrust in the mercy of God, and then, when the world sees me in this agony and bloody sweat, in this agony and bloody sweat would also see the angels of heaven ministering comforts unto me; so they would consider me in my *Peccavi,* and God in his *Transtulit,* me in my earnest confessions, God in his powerful absolutions, me drawn out of one sea of blood, the blood of mine own soul, and cast into another sea, the bottomless sea of the blood of Christ Jesus...

After these superb passages, Donne continues to say, essentially: What is my honor compared to glory being given to God?

...so they would know as well what God hath done for my soul, as what my soul and body have done against my God; so they would read me throughout, and look upon me altogether, I would join with Job, in his confident adjuration, *O earth, cover not thou my blood*; let all the world know all the sins of my youth, and of mine age too, and I would not doubt, but God should receive more glory, and the world more benefit, than if I had never sinned. This is that that exalts Job's confidence, he was guilty of nothing, that is, no such thing as they concluded upon, of nothing absolutely, because he had repented all. And from this, his confidence rises to a higher pitch than this, *Nex clamor, O earth cover not thou my blood, and let my cry have no place.*

...And truly, that is enough; I care not though all the world knew all my faults, I care not what they conclude of God's not granting my prayers, *My witness is in heaven.* To be condemned unjustly amongst men, to be ill interpreted in the acts of my religion, is a heavy case; but yet, I have a relief in all this, *My witness is in heaven.*

The first comfort is, because he, whom I rely upon, is in heaven... and so, *in procinctu,* in a readiness, in a willingness to come to my succour, so I might contemplate him in a judiciary posture, in a potestative, a sovereign posture, sitting, and consider him as able, as willing to relieve me. He is in heaven, and he sits in heaven, and then *habitat in cœlis,* he dwells in heaven, he is, and he is always there. Baal's priests could not always find him at home; Job's God, and our God is never abroad. He dwells in the heavens, and, (as it is expressed there) he dwells on. high; so high, that, (as it is there added) God humbles himself, to behold the things that are in heaven. With what amazedness must we consider the humiliation of God, in descending to the earth, lower than so, to hell, when even his descending unto heaven, is a humiliation? God humbles himself, when he beholds anything lower than himself, though Cherubims, though Seraphims, though the human nature, the body of his own, and only eternal Son; and yet he beholds; considers, studies us, worms of the earth, and no men.

This then is Job's, and our first comfort, *Quia in cælis,* because he is in heaven, and sits in heaven, and dwells in heaven, in the highest heaven, and so, sees all things...

Donne is now in his pastoral mode, working his way towards his close. He has courageously walked through this most enigmatic book of them all, Job, pushing life's toughest realities before us. Now he gives us commensurate reassurance in the depths and heights and inexhaustibility of God's love and mercy, in the blood that flowed from a voluntary giving, in love and for us.

...Now, if our own heart, our own conscience condemn us, this is shrewd evidence, says St. John; for mine own conscience, single, is a thousand witnesses against me. But then, (says the Apostle there) God is greater than the heart; for, (says he)

He knows all things; He knows circumstances of sin, as well as substance; and, that, we seldom know, seldom take knowledge of. If then mine own heart be a thousand, God,... if he be my witness, a witness for me, as he always multiplies in his ways of mercy, he is thousands of thousands, millions of millions of witnesses in my behalf, for *there is no condemnation*, no possible condemnation, *to them that are in him*; not, if every grain of dust upon the earth were an *Achitopel*, and gave counsel against me, not if every sand upon the shore were a *Rabshakeh*, and railed against me, not if every atom in the air were a Satan, an Adversary, an Accuser, not if every drop in the sea, were an Abaddon, an Apollyon, a Destroyer, there could be no condemnation, if he be my witness. If he be my witness, he proceeds thus in my behalf, his Spirit bears witness with my spirit, for mine inward assurance, that I stand established in his favour, and, either by an actual deliverance, or by some such declaration, as shall preserve me from fainting, if I be not actually delivered, he gives a farther testimony in my behalf. For, he is in heaven, and he sits in heaven, and he dwells in heaven, in the highest heaven, and sees all, and is a witness, and my witness; there is the largeness of our comfort.

But will all this come home to Job's end and purpose; that he need not care though all men knew all his faults, he need not care though God passed over his prayers, because God is his witness; what declarations soever he had in himself, would the world believe, that God testified in his behalf, when they saw his calamities multiplied upon lain, and his prayers neglected? If they will not, herein lies his and our final comfort, that he that is my witness, is in the highest heaven, there is no person above him, and therefore he that is my witness, is my judge too. I shall not be tried by an arbitrary court, where it may be wisdom enough to follow a wise leader, and think as he thinks. I shall not be tried by a jury, that had rather I suffered, than they fasted, rather I lost my life, than they lost a meal, Nor tried by peers, where honour shall be the Bible. But I shall be tried by the King himself, than which no man can propose a nobler trial, and that King shall be the King of Kings too; for he who in the first of the Revelation, is called *the faithful Witness*, is, in the same place, called *The Prince of the Kings of the earth*; and, as he is there produced as a *Witness*, so, he is ordained to be the *Judge of the quick and the dead*, and so, *all judgement is committed to him*. He that is my Witness, is my Judge, and the same person is my Jesus, my Saviour, my Redeemer; he that hath taken my nature, he that hath given me his blood. So that he is my Witness, in his own cause, and my Judge, but of his own Title, and will in me preserve himself; he will not let that nature that he hath invested, perish, nor that treasure which he hath poured out for me, his blood, be ineffectual. My Witness is in Heaven, my Judge is in Heaven, my Redeemer is in Heaven, and in them, who are but One, I have not only a constant hope, that I shall be there too, but an evident assurance, that I am there already, in his Person...

PREACHED AT WHITEHALL, THE FIRST FRIDAY IN LENT, 1622/3

This sermon is remarkable in many respects but perhaps especially in this: Donne seems presciently speaking to our age, an era which has discovered the value of mental health and the necessity of emotional expression to live in full well-being. Donne's text is the shortest verse in the Bible, "Jesus wept." And such a topic in the mind and imagination of such a poetic and rhetorically-gifted preacher! As he will say, "There is not a shorter verse in the Bible, nor a larger text."

Our excerpts here are not as long as the previous set, of the sermon on Job, but are not short either. There is much here that is worth working one's way through.

JOHN XI. 35. JESUS WEPT.

I AM now but upon the Compassion of Christ. There is much difference between his compassion and his passion, as much as between the men that are to handle them here. But *Lacryma passionis Christi est vicaria*: a great personage may speak of his passion, of his blood; my vicarage is to speak of his compassion and his tears. Let me chafe the wax, and melt your souls in a bath of his tears now, let him set to the great seal of his effectual passion, in his blood, then. It is a common place, I know, to speak of tears: I would you knew as well, it were a common practice to shed them. Though it be not so, yet bring St. Bernard's patience, *Libenter audiam, qui non sibi plausum, sed mihi planctum moveat;* Be willing to hear him, that seeks not your acclamation to himself, but your humiliation to his and your God; not to make you praise with them that praise, but to make you weep with them that weep, *And Jesus wept.*

The Masorites (the Masorites are the critics upon the Hebrew Bible, the Old Testament) cannot tell us, who divided the chapters of the Old Testament into verses; neither can any other tell us, who did it in the New Testament. Whoever did it seems to have stopped in an amazement in this text, and by making an entire verse of these two words, *Jesus wept,* and no more, to intimate that there needs no more for the exalting of our devotion to a competent height, than to consider how, and where, and when, and why *Jesus wept.* There is not a shorter verse in the Bible, nor a larger text. There is another as short; *Semper gaudete,* Rejoice evermore, and of that holy joy, I may have leave to speak here hereafter, more seasonably, in a more festival time, by my ordinary service. This is the season of general compunction, of general mortification, and no man privileged, for *Jesus wept.*

Donne notes that we see three times that Jesus wept: here, for Lazarus, as for a friend – human tears. When he looked upon Jerusalem, and foretold its fall, weeping for national calamity – prophetic tears. In the Garden before his Passion, weeping for sin and those who would not respond to his sacrifice – what he calls Pontifical tears, meaning related to sacrifice.

The tears of the text are as a spring, a well, belonging to one household, the sisters of Lazarus: the tears over Jerusalem, are as a river, belonging to a whole country; the tears upon the cross, are as the sea, belonging to all the world; and though literally there fall no more into our text, than the spring, yet because the spring flows into the river, and the river into the sea, and that wheresoever we find that Jesus wept, we find our text, (for our text is but that, *Jesus wept*) therefore by the leave and light of his blessed Spirit, we shall look upon those lovely, those heavenly eyes, through this glass of his own tears, in all these three lines, as he wept here over Lazarus, as he wept there over Jerusalem, as he wept upon the cross over all of us. For so often Jesus wept.

And Donne will honor Jesus' weeping and his expression of his feelings and his depth of them, as he begins to work to a place where he will suggest that true manliness is able to openly express grief and to weep:

He wept as man doth weep, and he wept as a man may weep; for these tears were *Testes naturæ, non Indices diffidentiæ*, they declared him to be true man, but no distrustful, no inordinate man. In *Job* there is a question asked of God, *Hast thou eyes of flesh, and doest thou see, as man sees?* Let this question be directed to God manifested in Christ, and Christ will weep out an answer to that question, I have eyes of flesh, and I do weep as man weeps. Not as sinful man, not as a man, that had let fall his bridle, by which he should turn his horse: not as a man that were cast from the rudder, by which he should steer his ship: not as a man that had lost his interest and power in his affections, and passions; Christ wept not so. Christ might go farther that way, than any other man: Christ might ungirt himself, and give more scope and liberty to his passions, than any other man: both because he had no original sin within to drive him, no inordinate love without to draw him, when his affections were moved; which all other men have.

Donne then continues his build-up by working through a few qualifications, considering sorts of weeping that come only from self-interest or self-indulgence, and the soul-danger that they are. Donne points out that Jesus did not weep in these ways, yet, nonetheless, Donne argues that suppressing true grief and affections is a more telling symptom of a soul-unwellness than its opposite. Jesus, therefore, in being our model for this as well, if anything defaulted towards open expression. But Jesus is neither "indolent" — too hard or selfish to weep — nor "inordinate" — weeping for selfish or silly reasons.

Now though Christ were far from both [sorts of excesses Donne had described], yet he came nearer to an excess of passion, than to an indolence, to s senselessness, to a privation of natural affections. Inordinateness of affections may sometimes make men like some beasts; but indolence, absence, emptiness, privation of affections, makes any man at all times, like stones, like dirt... Self-love in man sinks deep: but yet... you see, the Apostle [Peter] in his order, casts the other sin lower , that is, into a worse place, *To be without natural affections.*

And thus, what Donne will get to, is that what Jesus showed in his weeping for Lazarus was a natural, healthy, human response to the grief of the family and friends:

For our case in the text, these men whom Jesus found weeping, and wept with them were none of his kindred: they were neighbours, and Christ had had a conversation, and contracted a friendship in that family; *He loved Martha, and her sister, and Lazarus,* says the Story: and he would let the world see that he loved them: for so... [those] argued that saw him weep, *Behold how he loved them;* without outward declarations, who can conclude an inward love? to assure that, *Jesus wept.*

The healthy-souled person weeps without shame; otherwise, what will God do when he comes to wipe all tears away?

To an inordinateness of affections it never came; to a natural tenderness it did; and so far as to tears; and then who needs be ashamed of weeping? *Look away far from me, for I will weep bitterly*, says Jerusalem in *Isaiah*. But *look upon me,* says Christ in the Lamentations, *Behold and see if ever there were any sorrow, any tears like mine...* They scourged him, they crowned him, they nailed him, they pierced him, and then blood came; but he shed tears voluntarily, and without violence: the blood came from their ill, but the tears came of from his own good nature: the blood was drawn, the tears were given. We call it a childish thing to weep... Christ made it an argument of his being man, to weep, for though the lineaments of man's body, eyes and ears, hands and feet, be ascribed to God in the Scriptures, though the affections of man's mind be ascribed to him, (even sorrow, nay repentance its self, is attributed to God) I do not remember that ever God is said to have wept: it is for man. And when God shall come to that last act in the glorifying of man, when he promises *to wipe all tears from his eyes*, what shall God have to do with that eye that never wept?

Donne works through some other examples of weeping for beloved who have died and various circumstances involved, returns to Lazarus to talk about how Jesus planned along to use his friend's death as an opportunity to set a sign pointing to his coming resurrection, and yet when they complained to him that he might have done something his love for them overcame him, and he wept.

...he wept in this respect too, *Quia non adhibita media*, because those means which in appearance might have saved his life, by his default were not used, for when he came to the house, one sister, *Martha*, says to him, *Lord if thou hadst been here, my brother had not died*; and then the other sister, *Mary*, says so too, *Lord if thou hadst been here, my brother had not died*: they all cry out, that he who only, only by coming, might have saved his life, would not come. Our Saviour knew in himself that he abstained to better purpose, and to the farther glory of God: for when he heard of his death, he said to his disciples, *I am glad for your sakes that I was not there*. Christ had certain reserved purposes which conduced to a better establishing of their faith, and to a better advancing of God's Kingdom, the working of that miracle. But yet because others were able to say to him, it was in you to have saved him, and he did not, even this *quia non adhibita media*, affected him; and *Jesus wept*.

He wept, *Etsi quatriduanus*, though they said unto him, *He hath been four days dead, and stinks*. Christ doth not say, there is no such matter, he doth not stink; but though he do, my friend shall not lack my help...

Donne then transitions and spends some time discussing Jesus' second sort of weeping, prophetically, for what would eventually befall Jerusalem when the Romans sacked it in 70 AD. And then he turns to Jesus' third sort of weeping, tears for sin. Notice the wonderful image that comes soon in this excerpt: Donne will argue that those who set forth to sail on Jesus' tears for sin, who participate by repentance in these tears, finds their true self, and their soul's home.

...There remain yet his third tears, his pontifical tears, which accompany his sacrifice; those tears we called the sea, but a sea which must now be bounded with a very little sand.

To sail apace through this sea; these tears, the tears of his Cross, were expressed by that inestimable weight, the sins of all the world. If all the body were eye, argues the apostle in another place; why, here all the body was eye; every pore of his body made an eye by tears of blood, and every inch of his body made an eye by their bloody scourges. And if Christ's looking upon *Peter*, made *Peter* weep, shall not his looking upon us here, with tears in his eyes, such tears in such eyes, springs of tears, rivers of tears, seas of tears, make us weep too? *Peter* who wept under the weight of his particular sin, wept bitterly; how bitterly wept Christ under the weight of all the sins of all the world? In the first tears, Christ's humane tears (those we called a spring) we fetched water at one house, we condoled a private calamity in another; *Lazarus* was dead. In his second tears, his prophetical tears, we went to the condoling of a whole nation; and those we called a river. In these third tears, his pontifical tears, tears for sin, for all sins (those we call a sea) here is *mare liberum*, a sea free and open to all;

every man may sail home, home to himself, and lament his own sins there.

I am far from concluding all to be impenitent, that do not actually weep and shed tears; I know there are constitutions, complexions, that do not afford them. And yet the worst epithet which the best poet could fix upon *Pluto* himself, was to call him *Illachrymabilis*, a person that could not weep. But to weep for other things, and not to weep for sin, or if not to tears, yet not to come to that tenderness, to that melting, to that thawing, that resolving of the bowels which good souls feel; this is a sponge (I said before, every man is a sponge) this is a sponge dried up into a pumice stone; the lightness, the hollowness of a sponge is there still, but (as the pumice is) dried in the Ætnas [flames] of lust, of ambition, of other flames in this world.

I have but three words to say of these tears of this weeping. What it is, what it is for, what it does; the nature, the use, the benefit of these tears, is all. And in the first, I forbear to insist upon *St. Basil's* metaphor, *Lachrymæ sudor animi male sani*; Sin is my sickness, the blood of Christ Jesus is my Bezar [a city of refuge in ancient Israel], tears is the sweat that that produceth. I forbear *Gregory of Nyssa's* metaphor too, *Lachryma sanguis cordis defœeatus*; tears are our best blood, so agitated, so ventilated, so purified, so rarified into spirits, as that thereby I become *idem spiritus*, one spirit with my God... This weeping then is but a true sorrow, (that was our first) and then, what this true sorrow is given us for, and that is our next consideration.

As water is in nature a thing indifferent, it may give life, (so the first living things that were, were in the water) and it may destroy life, (so all things living upon the earth, were destroyed in the water) but yet though water may, though it have done good and bad, yet water does now one good office, which no ill quality that is in it can equal, it washes our souls in baptism; so though there be good tears and bad tears, tears that wash away sin, and tears that are sin, yet all tears have this degree of good in them, that they are all some kind of argument of good nature, of a tender heart; and the Holy Ghost loves to work in wax, and not in marble...

Finally, Donne does a bit of summing up, and then comes to his conclusion by bringing this all home to our hearts, using images and figures of holy weeping.

The fathers have infinitely delighted themselves in this descant, the blessed effect of holy tears. He amongst them that remembers us, that in the old Law all sacrifices were washed, he means, that our best sacrifice, even prayer itself, receives an improvement, a dignity, by being washed in tears. He that remembers us, that if any room of our house be on fire, we run for water, means that in all temptations, we should have recourse to tears. He that tells us, that money being put into a basin, is seen at a farther distance, if there be water in the basin, then if it be empty, means also, that our most precious devotions receive an addition, a multiplication by holy tears. *St. Bernard* means all that they all mean in that, *Cor lachrymas nesciens durum, impurum,* a hard heart is a foul heart. Would you shut up the devil in his own channel, his channel of brimstone, and make that worse? *St. Jerome* tells the way, *Plus tua lachryma, &c.* Thy tears torment him more than the fires of hell; will you needs have holy water? truly, true tears are the holiest water. And for Purgatory, it is liberally confessed by a Jesuit, *Non minus efficax, &c.* One tear will do thee as much good, as all the flames of Purgatory. We have said more than once, that man is a sponge; and in *Codice scripta,* all our sins are written in God's book, says *St. Chrysostom*: if there I can fill my sponge with tears, and so wipe out all my sins out of that book, it is a blessed use of the sponge.

I might stand upon this, the manifold benefits of godly tears, long; so long, as till you wept, and wept for sin; and that might be very long. I contract all to this one, which is all: to how many blessednesses must these tears, this godly sorrow reach by the way, when as it reaches to the very extreme, to that which is opposed to it, to Joy? for godly sorrow is Joy. The words in *Job* are in the Vulgate, *Dimitte me ut planegam dolorem meum: Lord spare me awhile that I may lament my lamentable estate*: and so ordinarily the expositors that follow that translation, make their use of them. But yet it is in the original, *Lord spare me awhile, that I may take comfort*: that which one calls *lamenting*, the other calls *rejoicing*: to conceive true sorrow and true joy, are things not only contiguous, but continual; they do not only touch and follow one another in a certain succession, joy assuredly after sorrow, but they consist together, they are all one, joy and sorrow. *My tears have been my meat day and night*, says *David*: not that he had no other meat, but that none relished so well. It is a grammatical note of a Jesuit... that when it is said, *Tempus cantus, the time of singing is come*, it might as well be rendered out of the Hebrew, *Tempus plorationis, the time of weeping is come*; and when it is said, *Nomini tuo cantabo, Lord I will sing unto thy Name*, it might be as well rendered out of the Hebrew, *Plorabo, I will weep, I will sacrifice my tears unto thy Name.* So equal, so indifferent a thing is it, when we come to godly sorrow, whether we call it sorrow or joy, weeping or singing.

To end all, to weep for sin is not a damp of melancholy, to sigh for sin, is not a vapour of the spleen, but as *Monica's* confessor said still unto her, in the behalf of her son *St. Augustine, filius istarum lachrymarum*, The son of these tears cannot perish; so wash thyself in these three examplar baths of Christ's tears, in his humane tears, and be tenderly affected with humane accidents, in his prophetical tears, and avert as much as in thee lieth, the calamities imminent upon others, but especially in his pontifical tears, tears for sin, and I am thy confessor, *non ego, sed Dominus*; not I, but the Spirit of God himself is thy confessor, and he absolves thee, filius istarum lachrymarum, the soul bathed in these tears cannot perish: for this is *trina immersio*, that threefold dipping which was used in the primitive Church in baptism. And in this baptism, thou takest a new Christian name, thou who wast but a Christian, art now a regenerate

Christian; and as *Naaman* the leper came cleaner out of Jordan, than he was before his leprosy, (for his flesh came as the flesh of a child) so there shall be better evidence in this baptism of thy repentance, than in thy first baptism... Weep these tears truly, and God shall perform to thee, first that promise which he makes in *Isaiah, The Lord shall wipe all tears from thy face*, all that are fallen by any occasion of calamity here, in the militant church; and he shall perform that promise which he makes in the Revelation, *The Lord shall wipe all tears from thine eyes*, that is, dry up the fountain of tears; remove all occasion of tears hereafter, in the triumphant Church.

DEATH'S DUEL
PREACHED BEFORE KING CHARLES

25 February 1631

Donne preached this, his most famous sermon, just over a month before he died, on 31 March 1631. Donne was famous for his funeral sermons, surely some of his most moving orations, and, again, the pain of death was not far from his experience. While this sermon was not formally a funeral sermon, nonetheless Donne was not well, seems to have known he was near his end, and, indeed, later this sermon came to be considered his own funeral sermon. Not a few remarked how it seemed fitting that he should manage something thought impossible — to preach one's own funeral.

Donne's paragraphs are long by our current standards; but these are exceedingly long. So please forgive me, I have taken the liberty of inserting paragraph breaks along the way, when it seemed helpful. Again, our excerpts taken together make a fairly long overall excerpt, but it is worth the work. And the conclusion sets us in a good place to enter Holy Week.

I have included the fuller title page's content here, including a note to the reader from the original publisher in 1640.

Death's Duel,
or,
A Consolation to the Soul, against the dying Life, and living Death of the Body.

Delivered in a Sermon at White Hall, before the King's Majesty, in the beginning of Lent, 1630.

To the Reader.

THIS *Sermon was, by Sacred Authority, styled the Author's own funeral Sermon. Most fitly: whether we respect* [regarding either] *the time, or the matter. It was preached not many days before his death; as if, having done this, there remained nothing for him to do, but to die: And the matter is, of Death; the occasion and subject of all funeral Sermons. It has been observed of the Reverend Man, That his Faculty in Preaching continually increased: and, That as he exceeded others at first; so, at last he exceeded himself. This is his last Sermon; I will not say, it is therefore his best; because, all his were excellent. Yet thus much: A dying Man's words, if they concern our selves; do usually make the deepest impression, as being spoken most feelingly, and with least affectation. Now, whom does it not concern to learn, both the danger, and benefit of death? Death is every man's enemy, and intends hurt to all; though to many, he be occasion of greatest goods. This enemy we must all combat dying; whom he living did almost conquer; having discovered the utmost of his power, the utmost of his cruelty. May we make such use of this and other the like preparatives, That neither death, whensoever it shall come, may seem terrible; nor life tedious; how long soever it shall last.* *R.*

PSA. 68 VERS. 20. IN FINE. *AND UNTO GOD THE LORD BELONG THE ISSUES OF DEATH.* i.e. *FROM DEATH.*

BUILDINGS stand by the benefit of their foundations that sustain and support them, and of their buttresses that comprehend and embrace them, and of their contignations that knit and unite them. The foundations suffer them not to sink, the buttresses suffer them not to swerve, and the contignation and knitting suffers them not to cleave. The body of our building is in the former part of this verse. It is this: *He that is our God is the*

God of salvation; ad salutes, of salvations in the plural, so it is in the original; the God that gives us spiritual and temporal salvation too. But of this building, the foundation, the buttresses, the contignations, are in this part of the verse which constitutes our text, and in the three divers acceptations of the words amongst our expositors: *Unto God the Lord belong the issues from death*, for, first, the foundation of this building (that our God is the God of all salvation) is laid in this, that *unto* this *God the Lord belong the issues of death*; that is, it is in his power to give us an issue and deliverance, even then when we are brought to the jaws and teeth of death, and to the lips of that whirlpool, the grave. And so in this acceptation, this *exitus mortis*, this issue of death is *liberatio á morte*, a deliverance from death, and this is the most obvious and most ordinary acceptation of these words, and that upon which our translation lays hold, the *issues from death*.

And then, secondly, the buttresses that comprehend and settle this building, that he that is our God is the God of all salvation, are thus raised; *unto God the Lord belong the issues of death*, that is, the disposition and manner of our death; what kind of issue and transmigration we shall have out of this world, whether prepared or sudden, whether violent or natural, whether in our perfect senses or shaken and disordered by sickness, there is no condemnation to be argued out of that, no judgment to be made upon that, for, howsoever they die, *precious in his sight is the death of his saints*, and with him are the issues of death; the ways of our departing out of this life are in his hands. And so in this sense of the words, this *exitus mortis*, the issues of death, is *liberatio in morte*, a deliverance in death; not that God will deliver us from dying, but that he will have a care of us in the hour of death, of what kind soever our passage be. And in this sense and acceptation of the words, the natural frame and contexture doth well and pregnantly administer unto us.

And then, lastly, the contignation and knitting of this building, that he that is our God is the God of all salvations, consists in this, *Unto* this *God the Lord belong the issues of death*; that is, that this God the Lord having united and knit both natures in one, and being God, having also come into this world in our flesh, he could have no other means to save us, he could have no other issue out of this world, nor return to his former glory, but by death. And so in this sense, this *exitus mortis*, this issue of death, is *liberatio per mortem*, a deliverance by death, by the death of this God, our Lord Christ Jesus. And this is

Saint *Augustine's* acceptation of the words, and those many and great persons that have adhered to him. In all these three lines, then, we shall look upon these words, first, as the God of power, the Almighty Father rescues his servants from the jaws of death; and then as the God of mercy, the glorious Son rescued us by taking upon himself this issue of death; and then, between these two, as the God of comfort, the Holy Ghost rescues us from all discomfort by his blessed impressions beforehand, that what manner of death soever be ordained for us, yet this *exitus mortis* shall be *introitus in vitam*, our issue in death shall be an entrance into everlasting life. And these three considerations: our deliverance *à morte, in morte, per mortem*, from death, in death, and by death, will abundantly do all the offices of the foundations, of the buttresses, of the contignation, of this our building; that he that is our God is the God of all salvation, because *unto* this *God the Lord belong the issues of death.*

With such powerful images he opened the sermon, and then knit them together. A bit later and Donne seems to have taken a turn, to seem to us even dour in his estimation of what our lives are. But, as ever, when he draws near to the hardest realities, he also remembers God's determination to deliver us, and Christ's work to pull us up.

...That which we call life is but *hebdomada mortium*, a week of death, seven days, seven periods of our life spent in dying, a dying seven times over; and there is an end. Our birth dies in infancy, and our infancy dies in youth, and youth and the rest die in age, and age also dies and determines all. Nor do all these, youth out of infancy, or age out of youth, arise so, as the phoenix out of the ashes of another phoenix formerly dead, but as a wasp or a serpent out of a carrion, or as a snake out of dung. Our youth is worse than our infancy, and our age worse than our youth. Our youth is hungry and thirsty after those sins which our infancy knew not; and our age is sorry and angry, that it cannot pursue those sins which our youth did; and besides, all the way, so many deaths, that is, so many deadly calamities accompany every condition and every period of this life, as that death itself would be an ease to them that suffer them.

Upon this sense doth Job wish that God had not given him an issue from the first death, from the womb, *Wherefore thou hast brought me forth out of the womb? Oh that I had given up the ghost, and no eye seen me! I should have been as though I had not been*. And not only the impatient Israelites in their murmuring (*would to God we had died by the hand of the Lord in the land of Egypt*), but Elijah himself, when he fled from Jezebel, and went for his life, as that text says, under the juniper tree, requested that he might die, and said, *It is enough now, O Lord, take away my life*. So Jonah justifies his impatience, nay, his anger, towards God himself: *Now, O Lord, take, I beseech thee, my life from me, for it is better to die than to live*. And when God asked him, *Dost thou well to be angry for this?* he replies, *I do well to be angry, even unto death*. How much worse a death than death is this life, which so good men would so often change for death! But if my case be as Saint Paul's case, *quotidiè morior*, that I die daily, that something heavier than death fall upon me every day; if my case be David's case, *tota die mortificamur; all the day long we are killed*, that not only every day, but every hour of the day, something heavier than death fall upon me; though that be true of me, *Conceptus in peccatis, I was shapen in iniquity, and in sin did my mother conceive me* (there I died one death); though that be true of me, *Natus filius irae*, I was born not only the child of sin, but the child of wrath, of the wrath of God for sin, which is a heavier death: yet *Domini Domini sunt exitus mortis, with*

God the Lord are the issues of death; and after a Job, and a Joseph, and a Jeremiah, and a Daniel, I cannot doubt of a deliverance. And if no other deliverance conduce more to his glory and my good, yet he hath the keys of death, and he can let me out at that door, that is, deliver me from the manifold deaths of this world, the *omni die*, and the *tota die*, the every day's death and every hour's death, by that one death, the final dissolution of body and soul, the end of all.

But then is that the end of all? Is that dissolution of body and soul the last death that the body shall suffer (for of spiritual death we speak not now). It is not, though this be *exitus à morte*: it is *introitus in mortem*; though it be an issue from manifold deaths of this world, yet it is an entrance into the death of corruption and putrefaction, and vermiculation, and incineration, and dispersion in and from the grave, in which every dead man dies over again. It was a prerogative peculiar to Christ, not to die this death, not to see corruption. What gave him this privilege? Not Joseph's great proportion of gums and spices, that might have preserved his body from corruption and incineration longer than he needed it, longer than three days, but it would not have done it for ever.

What preserved him then? Did his exemption and freedom from original sin preserve him from this corruption and incineration? It is true that original sin hath induced this corruption and incineration upon us; if we had not sinned in Adam, *mortality had not put on immortalit* (as the apostle speaks), nor *corruption had not put on incorruption*, but we had had our transmigration from this to the other world without any mortality, any corruption at all. But yet since Christ took sin upon him, so far as made him mortal, he had it so far too as might have made him see this corruption and incineration, though he had no original sin in himself; what preserved him then?

Did the hypostatical union of both natures, God and man, preserve him from this corruption and incineration? It is true that this was a most powerful embalming, to be embalmed with the Divine Nature itself, to be embalmed with eternity, was able to preserve him from corruption and incineration for ever. And he was embalmed so, embalmed with the Divine Nature itself, even in his body as well as in his soul; for the Godhead, the Divine Nature, did not depart, but remained still united to his dead body in the grave; but yet for all this powerful embalming, his hypostatical union of both natures, we see Christ did die; and for all his union which made him God and man, he became no man (for the union of the body and soul makes the man, and he whose soul and body are separated by death as long as that state lasts, is properly no man). And therefore as in him the dissolution of body and soul was no dissolution of the hypostatical union, so there is nothing that constrains us to say, that though the flesh of Christ had seen corruption and incineration in the grave, this had not been any dissolution of the hypostatical union, for the Divine nature, the Godhead, might have remained with all the elements and principles of Christ's body, as well as it did with the two constitutive parts of his person, his body and his soul. This incorruption then was not in Joseph's gums and spices, nor was it in Christ's innocency, and exemption from original sin, nor was it (that is, it is not necessary to say it was) in the hypostatical union.

But this incorruptibleness of his flesh is most conveniently placed in that; *Non dabis, thou wilt not suffer thy Holy One to see corruption*; we look no further for causes or reasons in the mysteries of religion, but to the will and pleasure of God; Christ himself limited his inquisition in that *ita est, even so, Father, for so it seemeth good in thy sight.* Christ's body did not see corruption, therefore, because God had decreed it should not. The humble soul (and only the humble soul is the religious soul) rests himself upon God's purposes and the decrees of God which he hath declared and manifested, not such as are conceived and imagined in ourselves, though upon some probability, some verisimilitude; so in our present case Peter proceeds in his sermon at Jerusalem, and so Paul in his at Antioch. They preached Christ to have been risen without seeing corruption, not only because God had decreed it, but because he had manifested that decree in his prophet, therefore doth Saint Paul cite by special number the second Psalm for that decree, and therefore both Saint Peter and Saint Paul cite for it that place in the sixteenth Psalm; for when God declares his decree and purpose in the express words of his prophet, or when he declares it in the real execution of the decree, then he makes it ours, then he manifests it to us.

And therefore, as the mysteries of our religion are not the objects of our reason, but by faith we rest on God's decree and purpose–(it is so, O God, because it is thy will it should be so)–so God's decrees are ever to be considered in the manifestation thereof. All manifestation is either in the word of God, or in the execution of the decree; and when these two concur and meet it is the strongest demonstration that can be: when therefore I find those marks of adoption and spiritual filiation which are delivered in the word of God to be upon me; when I find that real execution of his good purpose upon me, as that actually I do live under the obedience and under the conditions which are evidences of adoption and spiritual filiation; then, so long as I see these marks and live so, I may safely comfort myself in a holy certitude and a modest infallibility of my adoption. Christ determines himself in that, the purpose of God was manifest to him; Saint Peter and Saint Paul determine themselves in those two ways of knowing the purpose of God, the word of God before the execution of the decree in the fulness of time. It was prophesied before, said they, and it is performed now, Christ is risen without seeing corruption.

Now, this which is so singularly peculiar to him, that his flesh should not see corruption, at his second coming, his coming to judgment, shall extend to all that are then alive; their flesh shall not see corruption, because, as the apostle says, and says as a secret, as a mystery, *Behold I shew you a mystery, we shall not all sleep* (that is, not continue in the state of the dead in the grave), *but we shall all be changed in an instant*, we shall have a dissolution, and in the same instant a redintegration, a recompacting of body and soul, and that shall be truly a death and truly a resurrection, but no sleeping in corruption; but for us that die now and sleep in the state of the dead, we must all pass this posthume death, this death after death, nay, this death after burial, this dissolution after dissolution, this death of corruption and putrefaction, of vermiculation and incineration, of dissolution and dispersion in and from the grave, when these bodies that have been the children of royal parents, and the parents of royal children, must say with Job, *Corruption, thou art my father, and to the worm, Thou art my mother and my sister.* Miserable riddle, when the same worm must be my mother, and my sister and myself! Miserable incest, when I must be married to my mother and my sister, and be both father and mother to my own mother and sister, beget and bear that worm which is all that miserable penury; when my mouth shall be filled with dust, and the *worm shall feed, and feed sweetly* upon me; when the ambitious man shall have no satisfaction, if the poorest alive tread upon him, nor the poorest receive any contentment in being made equal to princes, for they shall be equal but in dust. *One dieth at his full strength, being wholly at ease and in quiet; and another dies in the bitterness of his soul, and never eats with pleasure; but they lie down alike in the dust, and the worm covers them.*

...And so have you that that belongs to the first acceptation of these words (*unto God the Lord belong the issues of death*); That though from the womb to the grave, and in the grave itself, we pass from death to death, yet, as Daniel speaks, *the Lord our God is able to deliver us, and he will deliver us.*

And so we pass unto our second accommodation of these words (*unto God the Lord belong the issues of death*); that it belongs to God, and not to man, to pass a judgment upon us at our death, or to conclude a dereliction on God's part upon the manner thereof.

Throughout this sermon, Donne is treading in dark and grey winter seas, but his confidence in God is commensurately strong.

But whether the gate of my prison be opened with an oiled key (by a gentle and preparing sickness), or the gate be hewn down by a violent death, or the gate be burnt down by a raging and frantic fever, a gate into heaven I shall have, for from the Lord is the cause of my life, and *with God the Lord are the issues of death.* And further we carry not this second acceptation of the words, as this *issue of death* is *liberatio in morte,* God's care that the soul be safe, what agonies soever the body suffers in the hour of death.

But pass to our third part and last part: As this issue of death is *liberatio per mortem,* a deliverance by the death of another. *Sufferentiam Job audiisti, et vidisti finem Domini,* says Saint *James, You have heard of the patience of Job,* says he: all this while you have done that, for in every man, calamitous, miserable man, a *Job* speaks. Now, *see the end of the Lord,* sayeth that apostle, which is not that end that the Lord proposed to himself (salvation to us), nor the end which he proposes to us (conformity to him), but *see the end of the Lord,* says he, the end that the Lord himself came to, death, and a painful and a shameful death. But why did he die? and why die so? *Quia Domini Domini sunt exitus mortis* (as Saint *Augustine,* interpreting this text, answers that question), because to this *God our Lord belonged the issues of death. Quid apertius diceretur?* says he there, what can be more obvious, more manifest than this sense of these words?

In the former part of this verse it is said, He that is *our God is the God of salvation; Deus salvos faciendi,* so he reads it, the God that must save us. Who can that be, says he, but *Jesus*? For therefore that name was given him because he was to save us. And to this *Jesus*, says he, this Saviour, *belong the issues of death; Nec oportuit eum de hac vita alios exitus habere quam mortis:* being come into this life in our mortal nature, he could not go out of this life any other way but by death. *Ideo dictum*, says he, therefore it is said, *to God the Lord belonged the issues of death; ut ostenderetur moriendo nos salvos facturum,* to show that his way to save us was to die. And from this text doth Saint *Isidore* prove that Christ was truly man (which as many sects of heretics denied, as that he was truly God), because to him, though he were *Dominus Dominus* (as the text doubles it), God the Lord, yet to *him, to God the Lord belonged the issues of death; oportuit eum pati*; more cannot be said than Christ himself says of himself; *These things Christ ought to suffer*; he had no other way but death: so then this part of our sermon must needs be a passion sermon, since all his life was a continual passion, all our Lent may well be a continual Good Friday.

Christ's painful life took off none of the pains of his death, he felt not the less then for having felt so much before. Nor will any thing that shall be said before lessen, but rather enlarge the devotion, to that which shall be said of his passion at the time of due solemnization thereof. Christ bled not a drop the less at the last for having bled at his circumcision before, nor will you a tear the less then if you shed some now. And therefore be now content to consider with me how *to this God the Lord belonged the issues of death.*

That God, this Lord, the Lord of life, could die, is a strange contemplation; that the Red Sea could be dry, that the sun could stand still, that an oven could be seven times heat and not burn, that lions could be hungry and not bite, is strange, miraculously strange, but super-miraculous that God *could* die; but that God *would* die is an exaltation of that. But even of that also it is a super-exaltation, that God should die, must die, and *non exitus* (said Saint *Augustine*), God the Lord had no issue but by death, and *oportuit pati* (says Christ himself), all this Christ ought to suffer, was bound to suffer; *Deus ultimo Deus*, says *David*, God is the God of revenges, he would not pass over the son of man unrevenged, unpunished. But then *Deus ultionum libere egit* (says that place), the God of revenges works freely, he punishes, he spares whom he will. And would he not spare himself? he would not: *Dilectio fortis ut mors, love is strong as death;* stronger, it drew in death, that naturally is not welcome.

Si possibile, says Christ, *if it be possible, let this cup pass,* when his love, expressed in a former decree with his Father, had made it impossible. *Many waters quench not love.* Christ tried many: he was baptised out of his love, and his love determined not there; he mingled blood with water in his agony, and that determined not his love; he wept pure blood, all his blood at all his eyes, at all his pores, in his flagellation and thorns (*to the Lord our God belonged the issues of blood*), and these expressed, but these did not quench his love. He would not spare, nay, he could not spare himself. There was nothing more free, more voluntary, more spontaneous than the death of Christ. It is true, *libere egit,* he died voluntarily; but yet when we consider the contract that had passed between his Father and him, there was an *oportuit,* a kind of necessity upon him: all this *Christ ought to suffer.* And when shall we date this obligation, this *oportuit,* this necessity? When shall we say that began? Certainly this decree by which Christ was to suffer all this was an eternal decree, and was there any thing before that that was eternal?

Infinite love, eternal love; be pleased to follow this home, and to consider it seriously, that what liberty soever we can conceive in Christ to die or not to die; this necessity of dying, this decree is as eternal as that liberty; and yet how small a matter made he of this necessity and this dying? His Father calls it but a bruise, and but a bruising of his heel (*the serpent shall bruise his heel*), and yet that was, that the serpent should practise and compass his death. Himself calls it but a baptism, as though he were to be the better for it. I *have a baptism to be baptized with*, and he was in pain till it was accomplished, and yet this baptism was his death. The Holy Ghost calls it joy (*for the joy which was set before him he endured the cross*), which was not a joy of his reward after his passion, but a joy that filled him even in the midst of his torments, and arose from him; when Christ calls his *calicem* a cup, and no worse (*Can ye drink of my cup*), he speaks not odiously, not with detestation of it. Indeed it was a cup, *salus mundo*, a health to all the world. And *quid retribuam*, says *David, What shall I render to the Lord?* Answer you with *David, Accipiam calicem, I will take the cup of salvation*; take it, that cup is salvation, his passion, if not into your present imitation, yet into your present contemplation. And behold how that Lord that was God, yet could die, would die, must die for your salvation.

Donne now begins to work his way to his conclusion, turning to the hope we have in Christ, working hard to pull our hearts and imaginations to embrace it, and walking us into Christ's Passion to get us there.

Take in the whole day from the hour that Christ received the passover upon Thursday unto the hour in which he died the next day. Make this present day that day in thy devotion, and consider what he did, and remember what you have done. Before he instituted and celebrated the *Sacrament* (which was after the eating of the *passover*), he proceeded to that act of humility, to wash his disciples' feet, even *Peter's*, who for a while resisted him. In thy preparation to the holy and blessed *sacrament*, hast thou with a sincere humility sought a reconciliation with all the world, even with those that have been averse from it, and refused that reconciliation from thee? If so, and not else, thou hast spent that first part of his last day in a conformity with him. After the *Sacrament* he spent the time till night in *prayer*, in *preaching*, in *Psalms*: hast thou considered that a worthy receiving of the sacrament consists in a continuation of holiness after, as well as in a preparation before? If so, thou hast therein also conformed thyself to him; so Christ spent his time till night. At night he went into the garden to pray, and he prayed *prolixious*, he spent *much time* in prayer, how much? Because it is literally expressed, that he prayed there three several times, and that returning to his disciples after his first prayer, and finding them asleep, said, *Could ye not watch with me one hour*, it is collected that he spent three hours in prayer. I dare scarce ask thee whither thou wentest, or how thou disposedst of thyself, when it grew dark and after last night. If that time were spent in a holy recommendation of thyself to God, and a submission of thy will to his, it was spent in a conformity to him. In that time, and in those prayers, was his agony and bloody sweat. I will hope that thou didst pray; but not every ordinary and customary prayer, but prayer actually accompanied with shedding of tears and dispositively in a readiness to shed blood for his glory in necessary cases, puts thee into a conformity with him.

About midnight he was taken and bound with a kiss, art thou not too conformable to him in that? Is not that too literally, too exactly thy case, at midnight to have been taken and bound with a kiss? From thence he was carried back to *Jerusalem*, first to *Annas*, then to *Caiaphas*, and (as late as it was) then he was examined and buffered, and delivered over to the custody of those officers from whom he received all those irrisions, and violences, the covering of his face, the spitting upon his face, the blasphemies of words, and the smartness of blows, which that gospel mentions: in which compass fell that *gallicinium*, that crowing of the cock which called up *Peter* to his repentance. How thou passedst all that time thou knowest. If thou didst any thing that needest *Peter's* tears, and hast not shed them, let me be thy cock, do it now. Now, thy *Master* (in the unworthiest of his servants) *looks back upon thee*, do it now. Betimes, in the morning, so soon as it was day, the *Jews held a council* in the *high priest's hall*, and agreed upon their evidence against him, and then carried him to *Pilate*, who was to be his judge; didst thou accuse thyself when thou wakedst this morning, and wast thou content even with false accusations, that is, rather to suspect actions to have been sin, which were not, than to smother and justify such as were truly sins? Then thou spentest that hour in conformity to him; *Pilate* found no evidence against him, and therefore to ease himself, and to pass a compliment upon *Herod, Tetrarch of Galilee*, who was at that time at Jerusalem (because Christ, being a Galilean, was of *Herod's* jurisdiction), *Pilate* sent him to *Herod*, and rather as a madman than a malefactor; *Herod* remanded him (with scorn) to *Pilate*, to proceed against him; and this was about eight of the clock. Hast thou been content to come to this inquisition, this examination, this agitation, this cribration, this pursuit of thy conscience; to sift it, to follow it from the sins of thy youth to thy present sins, from the sins of thy bed to the sins of thy board, and from the substance to the circumstance of thy sins? That is time spent like thy Saviour's.

Pilate would have saved Christ, by using the privilege of the day in his behalf, because that day one prisoner was to be delivered, but they chose *Barabbas*; he would have saved him from death, by satisfying their fury with inflicting other torments upon him, scourging and crowning with thorns, and loading him with many scornful and ignominious contumelies, but they regarded him not, they pressed a *crucifying*. Hast thou gone about to redeem thy sin, by fasting, by alms, by disciplines and mortifications, in way of satisfaction to the justice of God? That will not serve that is not the right way; we press an utter crucifying of that sin that governs thee: and that conforms thee to Christ.

Towards noon *Pilate* gave judgment, and they made such haste to execution as that by noon he was upon the *Cross*. There now hangs that *sacred Body* upon the *Cross*, *rebaptized* in his own tears, and sweat, and *embalmed* in his own blood alive. There are those bowels of compassion which are so conspicuous, so manifested, as that you may see them through his wounds. There those glorious eyes grew faint in their sight, so as the *sun*, ashamed to survive them, departed with his light too. And then that *Son of God*, who was never from us, and yet had now come a new way unto us in assuming our nature, delivers that soul (which was never out of his Father's hands) by a new way, a voluntary emission of it into his Father's hands; for though *to this God our Lord belonged these issues of death*, so that considered in his own contract, he must necessarily die, yet at no breach or battery which they had made upon his *sacred Body* issued his soul; but *emisit*, he *gave up the ghost*; and as *God breathed a soul into the first Adam*, so this *second Adam breathed his soul into God, into the hands of God.*

There we leave you in that blessed dependency, to hang upon him that hangs upon the *Cross*, there *bathe* in his tears, there *suck* at his wounds, and *lie down* in peace in his grave, till he vouchsafe you a *resurrection*, and an *ascension* into that *Kingdom* which he *hath purchased for you* with the *inestimable price* of his *incorruptible blood.* AMEN.

HOLY WEEK

What we may call regular Lent transitions into the intense focus on the events leading to Jesus' Cross. Our pilgrimage takes on a new weight and sobriety.

PALM SUNDAY

A Prayer of Confession

The Palm Sunday liturgy begins seemingly triumphant, as we mark and enact how Jesus entered Jerusalem to cheers, people greeting him by waving palm branches, and electric expectations. The liturgy soon changes abruptly, and we are in Gethsemane as Jesus wrestles in prayer, just before the mob comes with swords and clubs to take him away.

The story is told as the Passion Gospel is read in parts in the sacred liturgy. And then we all — the people gathered, the congregation, we *each* it would be more proper to say — join in the harrowing cry, "Crucify him! Crucify him!"

Ouch. It is valid, necessary, a realization each year, but it hurts, as well I suppose it ought. But we are speaking what is rightly ours to say; we are taking our part.

And so, we may as well go all the way and admit

it and get it all out. Thus, the reading I have set for this day is Donne's Prayer of Confession. Now, Donne's is a rather strong confession, but, if we are honest, we all can pray along with him in this.

But also, there is a paradox in the spiritual life: a poignant awareness of one's sins need not be a sign or symptom of self-hatred or self-belittling. Indeed, quite the contrary: the more intimate our awareness of God's magnificence, his simple (in the best way, meaning full, whole, un-compromised) holiness, and even, yes, of the relentlessness of his love, and lavishness of his gift of grace, the more acutely aware we are of our shortcomings. Perhaps *because* we have come to know we are deeply loved and are created for so much more.

Forgive me, O Lord,
O Lord, forgive me my sins,
the sins of my youth,
and my present sins,
the sin that my parents cast upon me,
original sin,
and the sins that I cast upon my children,
in an ill example;
actual sins,
sins which are manifest to all the world,
and sins which I have so labored to hide from the world,
as that now they are hid from mine own conscience,
and mine own memory.

Forgive me my crying sins,
and my whispering sins,
sins of uncharitable hate,
and sins of unchaste love,
sins against thee and against thy power, O almighty Father,
against thy wisdom, O glorious Son,
against thy goodness, O blessed Spirit of God;
and sins against him and him,
against superiors and equals,
and inferiors;

and sins against me and me,
against mine own soul,
and against my body,
which I have loved better than my soul.

Forgive me, O Lord,
O Lord, in the merits of thy Christ and my Jesus,
thine anointed,
and my savior.

Forgive me my sins,
all my sins,
and I will put Christ to no more cost,
nor thee to more trouble,
for any reprobation or malediction that lay upon me,
otherwise than as a sinner.

Amen.

Holy Monday

Holy Sonnet XII

The Monday of Holy Week is simply known as Holy Monday (and the Tuesday as Holy Tuesday). There is no particular event in the biblical narrative leading up to Jesus' passion that happens on this day, but we do turn our attention to somber events to come.

Donne's Holy Sonnet XII displays a kind of humility for our species that would serve us well both spiritually and in relation to the non-human world as well. Donne notes the irony that the earth and beasts have not sinned and are not so mixed of heart and motive as we. In many cases, they are superior in strength. And yet, a wonder — they serve us. In many cases they submit to us.

All of this is Donne reflecting on a paradox of life, and on the honor that God gave to us humans. Ah, but in those two, especially the latter, Donne is setting up his final four lines, and setting us up that we might feel and appreciate the size and holy incongruity of Christ's giving himself to death.

Why are we by all creatures waited on?
Why do the prodigal elements supply
Life and food to me, being more pure than I,
Simpler and further from corruption?
Why brook'st thou, ignorant horse, subjection?
Why dost thou, bull and boar, so sillily
Dissemble weakness, and by one man's stroke die,
Whose whole kind you might swallow and feed
upon?
Weaker I am, woe's me, and worse than you,
You have not sinn'd, nor need be timorous.
But wonder at a greater, for to us
Created nature doth these things subdue,
But their Creator, whom sin, nor nature tied,
For us, His creatures, and His foes, hath died.

Holy Tuesday

The Crosse

Holy Tuesday, like Holy Monday, does not have a clear event in the Passion narrative of Jesus that falls upon it. Still, we are one day closer and thereby that step more intent on focusing our hearts and attention on Jesus' sacrifice.

Today I have set an excerpt from Donne's poem, The Crosse. Our excerpt is the first half of the poem. And I must confess I have taken another, and greater liberty, that of adding a line break after the first set of sixteen lines, where there is something of a thematic shift.

Donne lived in an era in which the Reformation energy was beginning to do something the Catholic hierarchy had, in essence, warned Luther it would do: continue to swing, with the force of a pendulum, into excess beyond the reforms Luther had in mind. In England, it would not be long until, for instance, the Puritans controlled Parliament and the public celebration of Christmas — even in churches and their worship — was outlawed. The English Civil War and much blood-letting were in store.

It has not come to all of that yet, but there's enough ominous energy about that one layer of meaning in this poem is Donne writing essentially an apology for crosses in churches, as devotional aids, and so on.

My favorites are lines fifteen and sixteen, just before the break: Who can undo the effect of Holy Water, crossed upon one's forehead when one enters the church for Holy Communion; the Holy Water being the water of baptism, reminding us of who and whose we are?

And then, the second sixteen: our bodies, sporting in water; the masts and yards on ships, allowing the body of the ship to connect to the power of the wind; the bodies of birds perpendicular to their wings in flight; the very earth on which we stand, marked in longitude and latitude: the cross is integral to life, an inevitable response simply to how things are.

Material crosses are useful and not to be feared, Donne continues, but, yes, of course, spiritual ones are better — something like coming before the Cross of Christ in prayer and contemplation. But the power of both brings us to that self-surrendering place such that we rejoice in the gift, and that which the Puritans feared — a Crucifix — takes on a whole new, paradoxical meaning.

SINCE Christ embraced the cross itself, dare I
His image, th' image of His cross, deny?
Would I have profit by the sacrifice,
And dare the chosen altar to despise?
It bore all other sins, but is it fit
That it should bear the sin of scorning it?
Who from the picture would avert his eye,
How would he fly his pains, who there did die?
From me no pulpit, nor misgrounded law,
Nor scandal taken, shall this cross withdraw,
It shall not, for it cannot; for the loss
Of this cross were to me another cross.
Better were worse, for no affliction,
No cross is so extreme, as to have none;
Who can blot out the cross, with th'instrument
Of God dew'd on me in the Sacrament?

Who can deny me power, and liberty
To stretch mine arms, and mine own cross to be?
Swim, and at every stroke thou art thy cross,
The mast and yard make one, where seas do toss.
Look down, thou spiest out crosses in small things;
Look up, thou seest birds raised on crossed wings;
All the globe's frame, and spheres, is nothing else
But the meridians crossing parallels.
Material crosses then, good physic be,
But yet spiritual have chief dignity.

These for extracted chemic medicine serve,
And cure much better, and as well preserve;
Then are you your own physic, or need none,
When still'd or purged by tribulation.
For when that cross ungrudged unto you sticks,
Then are you to yourself a Crucifix.

Spy Wednesday

Holy Sonnet XI

Naming Holy Wednesday *Spy Wednesday* is not an ancient tradition, but a modern innovation. Still, one can see the point: we are close enough to the cross now that there is an event from the narrative that reasonably falls to this day: one of Jesus' own betrayed him. Judas Iscariot went to the chief priests and offered to turn Jesus over to them for a price. The verb in Greek that is used about this is two words put together: one, the preposition *para*, which can mean *from* or *beside*. It features more happily in the word *paradox*, meaning two glories beside each other. But here it is attached to a verb meaning to give. To give beside, or over to one beside. It is often translated as *given over*.

So I have set Holy Sonnet XI for this day. This poem could easily have been put on Good Friday, but there is a bit of competition for that most somber of days, and I already have set three poems there.

Therefore, I ask you to use a bit of imagination on this day and, rather than despise Judas Iscariot with a facile scorn, perhaps realize that we so often do not stand up courageously for what is good, true, and beautiful. For what is just. To some degree, perhaps we do betray with an untimely laugh or a self-serving excusing of another's excesses or because the moment just did not seem like a good one, or a million whatever elses... dissembling comes all too easily. But even if we do not betray, we are too often a part of that silent and thereby complicit number who the Rev'd. Dr. Martin Luther King, Jr., for instance, named several decades ago. Perhaps we have never gone secretly to a dark rendezvous with the wrong side and accepted payment, but also perhaps we are not so far from the darkness of it all as we would like to tell ourselves.

One last thing: the careful reader will notice here that there is not, in this sonnet, permission to take any kind of vengeance on Jews for the events that came about on these next few days in Jesus' life. Europe's history of evil and violence directed at them in return for crucifying Jesus is not only one of the most grievously ironic twists of history but also is a long history: the events of the previous century may have been the worst of it, but they are hardly the whole of it. And perhaps Donne, knowing this older history well, works a different kind of wit here. The first two lines strike one as provocative: the reader assumes it is the voice of Jesus. But lines three and four shift that perspective. And lines five and six make clear that our own sins are enough, and that we have no business judging others.

Spit in my face, you Jews, and pierce my side,
Buffet, and scoff, scourge, and crucify me,
For I have sinn'd, and sinne', and only He,
Who could do no iniquity, hath died:
But by my death can not be satisfied
My sins, which pass the Jews' impiety:
They kill'd once an inglorious man, but I
Crucify him daily, being now glorified;
O let me then His strange love still admire:
Kings pardon, but He bore our punishment.
And Jacob came clothed in vile harsh attire
But to supplant, and with gainful intent:
God clothed Himself in vile man's flesh, that so
He might be weak enough to suffer woe.

THE HOLY TRIDUUM

Formally, Lent ended yesterday. Maundy Thursday night to Easter Vigil on Holy Saturday night (Easter Eve) form the Holy Triduum, the Holy Three Days, and are set apart from the rest in their own space of intense devotion.

Our pilgrimage, however, is to the Cross, and so as we honor these three most holy days and acknowledge them, we will continue our pilgrimage in its last stages.

For Maundy Thursday we will take that last step toward Jesus' Cross.

On Good Friday three sacred poems will give us ample opportunity for sitting before his Cross.

And while we will not here venture over into Easter (Eve or Day), we will stay in the story and let two Holy Sonnets lead us into the depth of the moment on Holy Saturday.

MAUNDY THURSDAY

The liturgy for Maundy Thursday includes foot-washing, following Jesus' example of humbling himself, taking off his outer garments and putting on the towel of a servant. The word *Maundy* derives from the Latin, meaning *command*, as Jesus told us that on that night he was giving us a new command: to love one another.

But later that same night he would be alone in the garden, praying from his deepest inner self. But there also he would be betrayed, carried off by a mob with torches and bludgeons, and hauled to a secret nighttime convening of a sham court that was determined to find a way to get the result they wanted.

Holy Sonnet XII

On this day, on these leaden, heavy-laden steps our souls take through these sobering stages of our pilgrimage, we have a sonnet that begins with a question apt to this moment and ends with a reflection on the beauty of his sacrifice, and its effect by means only of love.

What if this present were the world's last night?
Mark in my heart, O soul, where thou dost dwell,
The picture of Christ crucified, and tell
Whether His countenance can thee affright,
Tears in His eyes quench the amazing light,
Blood fills his frowns, which from His pierced head fell
And can that tongue adjudge thee unto hell,
Which pray'd forgiveness for His foes' fierce spite?
No, no; but as in my idolatry
I said to all my profane mistresses,
Beauty of pity, foulness only is
A sign of rigour; so I say to thee,
To wicked spirits are horrid shapes assign'd,
This beauteous form assures a piteous mind.

GOOD FRIDAY

Today our pilgrimage reaches its destination. This was also the destination of Christ's coming to earth — it is not, of course, the end of him, but it was the singular purpose for which he said he came; "my hour" he named it as relayed in John's Gospel.

This is the most somber day of the whole of the church's year: the vestments of the holy liturgy are black, with no relief of any kind. The altar is bare. A pre-consecrated Eucharist, the liturgy for which is spare in the extreme. And the most dramatic of all liturgies it always seems to me, when our Lord Jesus' body is presented on the wood on which was hung the world's salvation, and each person is granted the opportunity for the adoration of the cross, a personal and public opportunity to give homage, to say thank you.

Three poems will help us settle down and contemplate the day. The first is about the challenge (even in Donne's day, apparently) of being able to lose all other interests or responsibilities and become lost in sincere soul-participation and thanksgiving. The second is strong in giving attention to the paradoxes of the day. The third marks a rare but meaningful conjunction.

You might spread them through the holy three hours in whatever manner fits your circumstance and temperament. Or spread them over morning, midday, and evening. If you are unable to pause for the whole of the holy three hours, this arrangement may work well — the first setting up the day, the midday one being the most poignant and falling at the start of those hours, and the last being suited to a quiet evening's reflection. Whatever arrangement is best for you, may you find yourself before our Lord's Cross, gratitude filling your heart.

Good Friday, 1613. Riding Westward.

If I may be allowed a personal reflection: this is my favorite Donne poem of them all. I have to confess that I know the sentiment Donne expresses here all too well, and, conversely, I know what it is when one is able to set this most solemn holy day aside for meditation and prayer. Donne longs to face the East, to give reverence and honor to Jesus and his cross, as is customary especially during the holy three hours from noon until three, the hours in which he hung there, in which he died.

The first ten lines orient us to Donne's struggle and frustration. The first six are, as people say nowadays, gold. This was an era in which the spheres—the celestial bodies—were of significant philosophical and scientific debate. The final parts of Johannes Kepler's major work, *Epitome Astronomiæ Copernicanæ*, were published ten years before Donne's death, for instance. Donne plays off of the astronomy that is all the rage but applies it to whether our souls are able to stay the course of their best orbit.

Basically, he is saying that the soul that is led by devotion — time with and before God — is the one that is on a good and healthy course, in keeping with the purpose for which it exists. Others are tugged away by diverting energies, losing their path, and thereby stressed and hurried. Ah. I suspect we each know this feeling all too well. He continues in the next lines to suggest that we move because we give pleasure or necessity the highest priority, and perhaps they are that about which we care most.

In lines nine and ten Donne transitions to where he longs to be: giving adoration and gratitude before the Cross.

Then he takes us there, as he begins a series of reflections via various paradoxes and observations on the majestic, though tragic, reality of that sacrificial death. Lines twenty-one and -two give honor to Jesus who is greater than the earth and keeps the whole cosmos going in its patterns and rhythm. In lines twenty-three and -four, *antipodes* is the place directly opposite us on this sphere which we call earth (anti-podes, or opposite our feet). Mary is given her due in line thirty-two in the understanding from the early Fathers that Jesus' divinity came of his conception by the Spirit of the

Lord, and his sharing in our humanity from Mary, in whose womb he developed.

Finally, the last ten lines are prayer and intimate devotion.

Let man's soul be a sphere, and then, in this,
Th'intelligence that moves, devotion is,
And as the other spheres, by being grown
Subject to foreign motion, lose their own,
And being by others hurried every day,
Scarce in a year their natural form obey:
Pleasure or business, so, our souls admit
For their first mover, and are whirl'd by it.
Hence is't, that I am carried towards the west
This day, when my soul's form bends to the East.
There I should see a Sun by rising set,
And by that setting endless day beget;
But that Christ on His cross did rise and fall,
Sin had eternally benighted all.
Yet dare I almost be glad, I do not see
That spectacle of too much weight for me.
Who sees Gods face, that is self-life, must die;
What a death were it then to see God die?
It made His own lieutenant, Nature, shrink,
It made His footstool crack, and the sun wink.
Could I behold those hands, which span the poles,
And tune all spheres at once, pierced with those holes?
Could I behold that endless height, which is
Zenith to us and our Antipodes,
Humbled below us? or that blood, which is
The seat of all our soul's, if not of his,
Made dirt of dust, or that flesh which was worn

By God for His apparel, ragg'd and torn?
If on these things I durst not look, durst I
On His distressed Mother cast mine eye,
Who was God's partner here, and furnish'd thus
Half of that sacrifice which ransom'd us?
Though these things as I ride be from mine eye,
They're present yet unto my memory,
For that looks towards them; and Thou look'st towards me,
O Saviour, as thou hang'st upon the tree;
I turn my back to thee but to receive
Corrections till thy mercies bid thee leave.
O think me worth thine anger, punish me,
Burn off my rust, and my deformity,
Restore thine image, so much, by thy grace,
That thou mayst know me, and I'll turn my face.

Crucifying

This is the fifth sonnet of seven in what is known as a crown of sonnets: a series of sonnets in honor of someone, connected in that the last line of each is the first line of the next, thereby making a circle of honor, a crown. Donne was such the master of wit that a tightly-constraining form, when he accepted it, presented a challenge which seems to have brought out even more brilliance. Some scholars suggest he may have been playing off a way of praying the Rosary that was popular in his day and was addressed to the Virgin Mother.

Whatever the specific details, he entitled the overall work simply *La Corona* (The Crown), and then gave each sonnet after the first its own name, corresponding to the event in the life of Christ that it celebrates.

If you read *Christmas with John Donne*, then you may recall sonnets two-four of the inter-connected crown.

By miracles exceeding power of man,
He faith in some, envy in some begat,
For, what weak spirits admire, ambitious hate;
In both affections many to him ran,
But O! the worst are most, they will and can,
Alas! and do, unto th'Immaculate,
Whose creature Fate is, now prescribe a fate,
Measuring self-life's infinity to span,
Nay to an inch. Lo! where condemned he
Bears his own cross, with pain, yet by and by
When it bears him, he must bear more and die;
Now Thou art lifted up, draw me to Thee,
And at Thy death giving such liberal dole,
Moist with one drop of Thy blood my dry soul.

The Annunciation and Passion

It is a rare coincidence indeed, but occasionally Good Friday falls on March 25, nine months to the day before December 25, Christmas Day, the day we celebrate Christ's birth. March 25th is the Annunciation when the angel Gabriel was sent to the Virgin Mary, to tell her of her completely singular good favor, and she accepts the depths of the path given to her.

In the twentieth century this concurrence happened three times: 1910, 1921, and 1932. In the twenty-first, its only two occurrences have already passed: 2005 and 2016. The next occurrence will be 2157. But it happened in 1608 according to the Julian Calendar which ordered the years in Donne's England.

Not surprisingly, such an occasion — a feast, celebrating a birth, and a fast, commemorating a death, and both of the same man — was more paradox than Donne could allow to pass by unremarked. Which is all well for us, for the complexities and ambiguities of his poem put us deep in the center of the mystery of the unity to which the convergence of these seemingly disparate events – the beginning and (in a sense) the end of Christ's earthly life – is a pointer, a signpost.

Our excerpt is the first half of the poem. At the beginning "she" is the day; in line thirteen "she" is the Blessed Virgin: the switch happened in lines eleven and twelve. Or perhaps the distinction is not quite that clear after all.

In line three "a circle emblem" is a symbol of perfection or eternity.

The poem gives us a wonderfully suggestive, albeit profoundly sad, word that it is a shame to have lost: "orbity". Now obsolete but having meant bereavement due to loss of parents or children, and which I am told derives from the Latin *orbatus,* being the past participle of *orbare,* meaning "to bereave". The idea is of such depth of grief as to dislodge one's very foundation, casting one into orbit, cut loose, desperately alone.

Donne, alas, knew the pain and loss that send one into orbity too well. When he was but the tender age of four his father died. His wife, Anne, gave birth to twelve children: two were stillbirths and three died before the age of ten. At one point in his grief, Donne wrote a defense of suicide, but (happily) he drew back from that abyss. Anne died five days after giving birth to their twelfth child (one of the stillborn two); Donne's poignant 17th Holy Sonnet was written of his grief for her.

Two years before her death Donne had been ordained priest and was awarded an honorary doctorate in divinity from Cambridge University. Six years later he was made Dean of St Paul's Cathedral, where he served ten years, until his death, and where he became famous for his sermons, not least his funeral orations, which are moving, profound, and forthright. He holds back nothing, forcing us to face the reality that we all face death and dissolution. Even during these years of newly-found wealth and of meaningful work death was not done with him; one of his daughters died at age eighteen, and, as we have seen, he nearly died from an illness that beset him quickly.

So one can easily imagine that the concurrence in one day of the hope of the Annunciation and the taking on our sufferings of Good Friday would poignantly have spoken to Donne. And why not to each of us? The first two lines alone leave me breathless, and the seventh strikes me dumb with awe.

The going full circle is in the poem, of course, as well: the last line of our excerpt catches this:

"th'angels *Ave* [Gabriel greeting Mary] and *Consummatum est* [Jesus' 'It is finished' from the Cross]." It testifies to a theme that John, especially, brought forward in his Gospel: that Jesus knew all along that he was headed to the cross, the culmination and necessary act to spring a new start, a new creation. This moment was always where he was headed; in John's Gospel he referred to his as "my hour."

Tamely, frail body, abstain to-day; to-day
My soul eats twice, Christ hither and away.
She sees Him man, so like God made in this,
That of them both a circle emblem is,
Whose first and last concur; this doubtful day
Of feast or fast, Christ came, and went away;
She sees Him nothing, twice at once, who's all;
She sees a cedar plant itself, and fall,
Her Maker put to making, and the head
Of life at once not yet alive, yet dead;
She sees at once the Virgin Mother stay
Reclused at home, public at Golgotha.
Sad and rejoiced she's seen at once, and seen
At almost fifty, and at scarce fifteen.
At once a son is promised her, and gone.
Gabriel gives Christ to her, He her to John;
Not fully a mother, she's in orbity,
At once receiver and the legacy;
All this, and all between, this day hath shown,
Th' abridgement of Christ's story, which makes one—
As in plain maps, the furthest west is east—
Of th' angels *Ave,* and *Consummatum est.*

The Collect for Good Friday

ALMIGHTY God, we beseech thee graciously to behold this thy family, for the which our Lord Jesus Christ was contented to be betrayed, and given up into the hands of wicked men, and to suffer death upon the cross: who now liveth and reigheth with thee, in the unity of the Holy Ghost, ever one God, world without end. AMEN.

HOLY SATURDAY

What happened on this day can be a controversial discussion. The Medieval English church called the time between Jesus' death and his resurrection "the harrowing of hell": Jesus descending to the dead to liberate the righteous dead, leading them out in a train of victory. Think "...upon this rock I will build my church, and the gates of hell shall not prevail against it." It is not the church that is behind gates; it is the church (in the Person of Jesus) going forward and busting the gates.

The details are, admittedly, fuzzy. But two of the three ecumenical creeds used in the Anglican Church have this idea: the Apostles' Creed and the Athanasian Creed.

We have two sonnets set for this day. They are two of Donne's most famous. Neither one of them was written for the day, and they do not address the whole "hallowing" business.

The first does, however, put death on notice that its time is short, and its self-assurance mistaken. And the second is a wonderful prayer serving as a bit of closure to our pilgrimage.

Holy Sonnet X

Perhaps his most famous sonnet, known commonly as Death Be Not Proud, this one was written during Donne's years of intense loss and grief – a kind of riposte against death's insistent stealing from him. On this day of all days, we can say its last clause. Relish it.

Death, be not proud, though some have called thee
Mighty and dreadful, for thou are not so,
For those whom thou think'st thou dost overthrow,
Die not, poor Death, nor yet canst thou kill me;
From rest and sleep, which but thy pictures be,
Much pleasure; then from thee much more must flow,
And soonest our best men with thee do go,
Rest of their bones, and soul's delivery.
Thou'art slave to fate, chance, kings, and desperate men,
And dost with poison, war, and sickness dwell,
And poppy'or charms can make us sleep as well,
And better than thy stroke; why swell'st thou then?
One short sleep past, we wake eternally,
And death shall be no more; Death, thou shalt die.

Holy Sonnet XIV

Thank you for pilgriming with me, for your trust and your good heart. I hope this pilgrimage has given depth for reflection and insight to your Lent this year and will multiply your celebration on the morrow. The happy, happy Morrow. Yesterday the breaking free that Donne seeks in this sonnet was accomplished.

I offer this sonnet as a prayer — it is for me and perhaps a mete one for you as well — that all of this will forever stir your heart to its very core and move you to deep love: in Donne's language, to be enthralled, as you are ravished.

Batter my heart, three-person'd God, for you
As yet but knock, breathe, shine, and seek to mend;
That I may rise, and stand, o'erthrow me, and bend
Your force to break, blow, burn, and make me new.
I, like an usurped town, to another due,
Labour to admit you, but O, to no end,
Reason, your viceroy in me, me should defend,
But is captiv'd, and proves weak or untrue,
Yet dearly I love you, and would be loved fain,
But am betroth'd unto your enemy,
Divorce me, untie or break that knot again,
Take me to you, imprison me, for I
Except you enthrall me, never shall be free,
Nor ever chaste, except you ravish me.

* * *

SOURCES

Books:

Carey, John (ed. and introduction), *John Donne, The Major Works, including Song and Sonnets and sermons,* Oxford World's Classics, Oxford University Press, 2000.

Dent, J. M., (ed., introduction, and critical endmatter), *Everyman Complete English Poems of John Donne,* Everyman, Orion Publishing Group, Ltd., London, 1994.

Motion, Andrew, (introduction), *Devotions Upon Emergent Occasions and Death's Duel, with The Life of Dr. John Donne by Izaak Walton,* Vintage Spiritual Classics, Vintage Books, A Division of Random House, Inc., New York, 1999.

Rundell, Katherine, *Super Infinite, the Transformations of John Donne,* Farrar, Straus, and Giroux, New York, 2022.

Simpson, Evelyn M., ed. and introduction, *John Donne's Sermons on the Psalms and Gospels,* University of California Press, Berkeley and Los Angeles, California, 1991.

Online:

I am grateful for the excellent collection of Donne's sermons that are available online through Brigham Young University: https://lib.byu.edu/collections/john-donne-sermons/.

Printed in Great Britain
by Amazon

58853595R00128